Mercedes-Benz W201 (190)

THE COMPLETE STORY

OTHER TITLES IN THE CROWOOD AUTOCLASSICS SERIES

Mercedes-Benz W201 (190)

THE COMPLETE STORY

JAMES TAYLOR

THE CROWOOD PRESS

First published in 2020 by
The Crowood Press Ltd
Ramsbury, Marlborough
Wiltshire SN8 2HR

enquiries@crowood.com

www.crowood.com

British Library Cataloguing-in-Publication Data
A catalogue record for this book is available from the British Library.

ISBN 978 1 78500 733 0

Typeset by Jean Cussons Typesetting, Diss, Norfolk

Printed and bound in India by Parksons Graphics

CONTENTS

INTRODUCTION AND ACKNOWLEDGEMENTS

My first experience of a Mercedes 190 was a little unfortunate. After a breakdown in the family car somewhere deep in France, our travel insurers directed us to a small car hire place that proudly offered us the flagship of its fleet – a carburettor 190. Frankly, it was a bit small to accommodate four people plus holiday luggage, but we squeezed ourselves in and headed for the nearest autoroute.

It wasn't long before I began to realize that, although it was rather small and was the base model, this was a high-quality piece of machinery. I can still remember grinning as the car reeled in the miles, and wondering what the higher-spec, more expensive versions must be like. Two years later, I found out by buying a 190E automatic, which turned out to be a superb car, just as I had expected.

Many years and a few books about Mercedes cars later, I am still trying to think of a justification for buying another 190. In the mean time I have squirrelled away every scrap of information that has come my way about the cars, and there it all was when I decided to write this book. I hope it does these fine cars justice, although I'm quite happy to accept that there may be more to say about them one day. Historical information has a way of remaining hidden until chance events push it to the surface.

Lots of people made contributions to this book, although few of them probably realized they were doing so at the time. The Mercedes-Benz UK press office kept me informed about the evolution of the range in the 1980s and 1990s, and their counterparts at MBUSA helped out with some specific queries. Mercedes-Benz Classic provided further information and most of the illustrations. My own camera and Magic Car Pics supplied several others, and yet more came from various internet sources. A significant amount of information came from the *Gazette*, the excellent magazine of the Mercedes-Benz Club in the UK, and from *Mercedes Enthusiast* magazine, along with multiple foreign-language sources (and especially German ones) over the years.

James Taylor
Oxfordshire

TIMELINE

1982, December   Launch of 190 and 190E

1983, September   Launch of 190D; W201 range introduced to USA as 190E 2.3 and 190D 2.2. Five-speed option

1984, September   Introduction of 190E 2.3-16

1985, May   Launch of 190D 2.5

1985, September   First European models with catalytic converter option

1985, November   Half-millionth W201 built

1986, April   190E 2.6 available

1986, spring   190D 2.5 Turbo for USA

1986, September   European KAT (with catalytic converter) and RÜF (pre-prepared for catalytic converter) models introduced. 190E 2.3 available in Europe

1987, September   190D 2.5 Turbo for markets outside USA

1988, spring   Millionth W201 built

1988, September   Major facelift revealed. 190E 2.5-16 introduced

1989, March   190E 2.5-16 Evolution announced

1989, September   Catalytic converters now standard world-wide. Sportline options introduced

1990, March   190E 2.5-16 Evolution II announced

1991, January   190E 1.8 replaces carburettor 190. 190E renamed 190E 2.0

1992, March   First run-out editions announced

1992, October   Final specification changes

1993, August   Final production in Germany

CHAPTER ONE

BACKGROUND AND DEVELOPMENT

The way Mercedes-Benz likes to tell the story, the decision to proceed with a smaller Mercedes saloon was taken at the Geneva motor show in March 1973. This was some months before the first Oil Crisis, which undoubtedly gave the idea a higher priority than it might otherwise have had. It was also some time before the popularity of the Volkswagen Golf demonstrated the possibilities of such a car, but just over a year after the French Renault company had shown the way forward with their new Renault 5 'supermini'.

Exactly what the parties to that 1973 decision had in mind is not clear; quite probably, they all had their own different vision of what form a new smaller Mercedes might take. However, by the end of the year, the focus at Mercedes-Benz headquarters in Stuttgart was on a much more immediate problem. In October, the members of the Organization of Arab Petroleum Exporting Countries (OPEC) announced

an oil embargo, targeted at those nations that were perceived to have supported Israel during the Yom Kippur War. Among the nations subject to the oil embargo was the USA, which was a major export market for Mercedes cars. By the time the embargo was lifted, in 1974, the price of oil from the OPEC countries had risen by 400 per cent, with a consequent knock-on effect on petrol and diesel prices.

The fall-out from this was far-reaching. As far as Mercedes was concerned, it was clear that cars with high fuel consumption were going to become more difficult to sell – and that really meant most of the models they then had in production. There was no such thing as a small or frugal Mercedes at the time, despite the fact that the company was a world leader in diesel passenger cars, which had much better fuel economy than their petrol equivalents. Without a small model that was economical to run, Mercedes was

A very early 190, pictured in a typically English setting. Britain would become the 190's largest European market outside West Germany.

going to lose sales rapidly to other companies that did have such models in their catalogues. The need for that small model had suddenly become critical to the future of the company.

MERCEDES IN THE 1970s

When the Oil Crisis struck, in 1973–1974, Mercedes had three main car ranges and was universally perceived as a maker of large and prestigious models. It had a world-wide reputation for its research into vehicle safety and for incorporating safety features into its cars, and for building vehicles that were reliable and durable – even if they were also expensive. The taxi driver who saved up to buy a Mercedes saloon did so in the knowledge that it would probably last him for most of his working life and was therefore worth every last Deutschmark of its high initial cost.

The smallest of the Mercedes models in the early 1970s was a medium-sized saloon with engines of between 2.0 litres and 3.0 litres. There were six-cylinder models (known internally as W114 types) and four-cylinder models (W115 types), and equipment levels varied from spartan (which appealed to the taxi driver) to quite luxurious. A prestigious two-door coupé range had been spun off from the basic saloon design.

The flagship Mercedes saloon was known as the S Class, and was an engineering *tour de force* that had been introduced in 1972. Larger than the medium-sized models, the W116 models could be had with either the standard wheelbase, which gave generous interior space, or a long wheelbase, which gave lounging room in the rear and was suited to chauffeur-driven duties. Engines ranged from a 2.8-litre six-cylinder up to a 4.5-litre V8 (and from 1975 there would be a 6.9-litre V8 as well). These cars were considered on a par with models from Rolls-Royce, and many knowledgeable people actually considered them to be better.

There was then the SL (R107) sports range of luxurious two-seat roadsters, which shared their engines with the S Class. Closely related was the SLC (C107) range, which was really a long-wheelbase SL with a fixed coupé roof and four seats. The SLC was promoted as the most stylish of the Mercedes models.

The medium-sized Mercedes in the first half of the 1970s was the W114/W115 range; it gave way in 1976 to the W123.

The flagship Mercedes for most of the 1970s was the W116 S Class.

The third Mercedes range was the R107 SL sports model; there was a long-wheelbase SLC coupé derivative as well.

These cars, and their predecessors in the 1960s and 1950s, had created a strong public image for Mercedes as a maker of expensive and aspirational vehicles with large-capacity engines. The new G-Wagen off-road vehicle that was introduced in 1979 only served to reinforce that image. As a result, Mercedes would have to organize a major publicity campaign when its new compact saloon was released, in order to convince the buying public that this new type was indeed a true Mercedes. For many people, it would take years to come to terms with the smaller and less expensive model.

THE BRIEF FOR THE W201

The enactment of new regulations relating to the overall fuel consumption of a car maker's products by the US Congress during 1975 made it even clearer that Mercedes would need a more frugal model in its range. The so-called CAFE rules (about which there is more in Chapter 6) threatened Mer-

cedes with corporate fines if they failed to comply with miles-per-gallon figures that would be not only legally enforced but would also get progressively tighter. As a result, by the autumn of 1976, a formal development project had been established for a new and compact Mercedes saloon. It was known internally as the W201 model.

The overall responsibility for developing the W201 would fall to Werner Breitschwerdt, who was appointed as the new head of Mercedes' research and development division in 1977. Known for his innovative work (he had been behind the ABS development programme), he was the ideal man to lead the teams working on the new compact Mercedes.

The brief for the W201 had certain very clear requirements from the start. The new car must not compromise any of the traditional Mercedes qualities. It must incorporate all the established marque characteristics of solid build quality, maximum safety and modern technology. Its comfort and long-distance touring abilities had to be as good as those of the flagship S Class; durability and longevity had to be comparable, as did the ease of maintenance and repair.

Werner Breitschwerdt was appointed as the new head of Mercedes research and development in 1977.

Breitschwerdt with an example of the W201 Mercedes, which benefited so much from his clear-thinking approach.

Critically, its fuel consumption had to be much lower than that of the existing medium-sized Mercedes, and that meant a reduction in both size and weight. The design team would have to find the best compromise between interior space and exterior dimensions.

From quite early on, it became clear that this new model would be a traditional three-box saloon rather than a two-box hatchback design, which at this stage was perceived as much more down-market than Mercedes wanted to be – despite the undoubted success of Volkswagen's Golf. There were no plans for estate or coupé derivatives – the car was drawn up strictly as a four-door saloon – although, in later years, there would be experiments with derivatives.

While the designers and engineers worked on the shape and structure of the new compact saloon, the sales and marketing teams set about identifying the likely customer base. They decided that Mercedes needed to look at attracting a new group of buyers, rather than trying to persuade their existing customers to downsize – although they accepted that this might happen in some cases. The new model needed to appeal to existing buyers of small BMWs (the 3 Series, then available only in two-door saloon form), small Audi models (the four-door 80 saloon) and the new Saab 900, which was redeveloped in 1978 specifically for the USA.

Lower down the scale, it should also tempt owners of hatchbacks such as the Volkswagen Golf to trade up. Their top priority as a target owner group was those aged under 30.

The concept came together for the first time in 1978, and it is interesting to compare the dimensions that were determined for the new compact saloon with those of the then-current medium-sized Mercedes – which by this time was the W123 range that had replaced the W114 and W115 models in 1976. The W201 was to be 305mm (12in) shorter overall than a W123, with a wheelbase that was 130mm (just over 5in) shorter. It was to be 108mm (4.25in) narrower, 88mm (3.46in) less tall, and, by the time production began, it would weigh over 250kg (551lb) less than the entry-level 200 model of the W123 saloon range. The changes in approach that were needed at Mercedes to meet the W201 brief were simply enormous.

DRIVETRAIN

An important early consideration was whether the small saloon should have the traditional Mercedes rear-wheel drive or should switch to the front-wheel drive that was so much favoured for smaller cars. The company had in fact developed a front-wheel-drive system around a decade and a half earlier for the W118 'small' Mercedes (see below). Although this car never went into production, the development process had shown that the system made bet-

THE EARLIER COMPACT MERCEDES

The W201 was not Mercedes' first post-war attempt to create a smaller saloon model. In 1953, they had started work on the W122 project, which aimed to deliver a four-door saloon that was 15 to 20 per cent smaller than the latest Ponton saloons and shared some of their visual character. However, the car was cancelled in 1956 when work began on the W111/W112 Fintail saloons that would have a very different visual aspect.

The W122 was designed as a smaller Mercedes saloon at the time of the Pontons, but did not make production.

An alternative W122 design shows a progression towards the newer Fintail styling, especially in the rear pillar treatment.

A second project for a smaller Mercedes was started in 1958. Known as the W118, it was developed under R&D chief Ludwig Kraus as a front-wheel-drive car with a four-cylinder 1.5-litre 'boxer' engine. A later development saw the introduction of a 1.7-litre in-line four-cylinder engine that had started life at Mercedes for a military project, and this version became known as the W119. By 1962, however, Mercedes had decided that there was no market for it.

Daimler-Benz had acquired a majority shareholding in the ailing Auto Union company during 1958, and in 1959 assumed full control. Auto Union were desperately in need of new models. Mercedes seconded Klaus Ludwig as deputy managing director and technical director in 1963, to oversee the creation of these. Ludwig proposed using the 1.7-litre engine from the W119 in the latest Auto Union bodyshell (which then had an antiquated two-stroke engine), and this duly appeared in 1965 as an Audi, using a name last seen on cars in 1939. In the mean time, Daimler-Benz had sold Auto Union to Volkswagen, and so the engine intended for their own medium-sized car actually kick-started the career of a major rival.

TOP: **The W118 was to be a compact four-door saloon that would fit below the medium-sized Fintails in the Mercedes range.**

MIDDLE: **The other side of the styling model shows that a two-door version was also envisaged.**

BOTTOM: **Despite its compact size, the W118 had good interior space, thanks to a front-wheel-drive layout.**

ter use of interior space and was the best solution for a car that weighed no more than 900kg unladen. However, getting below that 900kg (1,984lb) mark in a car with all the traditional Mercedes qualities was expecting a lot – a 123-series saloon typically weighed somewhere around 1,350kg (2,976lb).

Mercedes did not in fact dismiss front-wheel drive until 1979, and probably some of the early development 'mules' had it. A factor in the eventual choice of rear-wheel drive was that the W201 was being designed with a view to component sharing with the next generation of medium-sized Mercedes saloons. Front-wheel-drive components in the smaller car would have been incompatible with the rear-wheel-drive layout that was firmly in the frame for the larger one.

STYLING

On the styling side of the Mercedes house, there was another new name at the top. In 1975, Bruno Sacco had taken over from the long-serving Friedrich Geiger as head of styling. Italian by birth, Sacco had been with Mercedes since 1958, and had already embarked on creating a new and modern

design language for the marque. This would be seen first in the W126 S Class introduced in 1979, and was characterized by simple, sculpted and unadorned lines that had a classical elegance about them. Sacco believed in what he described as both vertical and horizontal integration for car styling: by vertical integration, he meant that each new model should be clearly related to the one it replaced; horizontal integration meant that all the models in a manufacturer's range should have a family resemblance. So it was that his design for the W201 picked up some of the themes already seen in the W126 and, later, the W124 medium-sized saloons of 1984 would embody the same characteristics.

The earliest designs for the new compact saloon were prepared as scale models in late 1977, as it was important to have some ideas to work on even before the final dimensions were agreed. These showed a focus on aerodynamics, which would of course be important in minimizing fuel consumption at higher speeds. At least one early design integrated the traditional Mercedes grille shape into the front panel, but eventually the front-end design was drawn up to give a close family resemblance to the W126 range – following Sacco's rules of 'horizontal integration' – with flush-fitting light units that incorporated auxiliary driving lamps alongside the headlights. The bumpers and aprons also resembled their

In charge of styling for the W201 was Bruno Sacco, pictured here in later years with a scale model of the car.

This early scale model for the W201 was created in Sacco's studio in 1977, before the full set of ideas for the new model had come together.

Even though the new model was to be a compact saloon, the lines of the 1977 model deliberately suggested a larger car.

W126 counterparts, while the wraparound front and rear indicators had the ribbed lenses that were now a Mercedes trademark and had originally been designed to prevent road dirt building up and obscuring the lights.

Aerodynamic considerations ensured that the windscreen would be more steeply raked than its W126 equivalent. It was also arranged with a minimum of intrusion from the A pillars, to which it was bonded, and this added to the car's structural rigidity and did away with the traditional rubber seal that prevented a smooth airflow over the top of the car. Plastic deflector panels on the pillars were designed to duct rainwater up and over the roof and to prevent it from obscuring the side windows, and channels on the roof directed that rainwater towards the back of the car. The rear edge of the bonnet was curved gently upwards to aid clean airflow, and to prevent the wiper arm – there was only one – creating wind noise when in its parked position. The production W201 would have a Cd of 0.33, which was lower than any previous model from Mercedes.

There was an inescapable logic to Mercedes design. The doors opened by pulling the handle – a natural and intuitive movement – and had a rounded shape to reduce the risk of injury.

New to Mercedes, the aerodynamic chamfer at the tops of the rear wings was initially controversial.

The trailing edge of the bonnet curved upwards to improve airflow and conceal the single wiper blade.

The polycarbonate wheel trims were simple and aerodynamic in design, with radial cooling slots for the brakes.

The alternative alloy wheel was also drawn up with a flat, aerodynamic face and radial cooling slots.

Interestingly, the decision was taken not to go for flush glazing of the side windows (which Audi would introduce in 1982 on its third-generation 100 model). Mercedes reasoned that the predicted 1 per cent improvement in aerodynamics would be gained only at the cost of complications in assembly and repair. Even so, they made the side window glass as flush as they reasonably could, and on the W201 it was inset by just 6mm, a dimension that becomes more significant when compared to the 11.5mm inset of the side glass on a W123 saloon.

The most obvious attention to aerodynamics was evident at the rear, but it was only visible from some angles. The lower body was wedge-shaped, with a rising belt line that tapered more steeply upwards than was immediately apparent. The boot line was noticeably higher than on earlier Mercedes models, partly to improve airflow but also to compensate for the fact that the boot was short in comparison with the company's other saloons. There was an angled section to manage the airflow at the rear of the roof just above the back window, and the tops of the rear wings had a marked chamfer for the same reason. This feature in particular would prove controversial. It was toned down to become more rounded on the W124 medium-sized saloons that followed the W201, which were nonetheless closely similar in shape.

Another element of the W201's appearance that caused controversy was the design of the wheels. The standard fit was to be a 14-inch steel disc type and Sacco's team designed a flush-fitting trim that incorporated turbine-like slots to aid brake cooling. The trims were designed to reduce aerodynamic drag, but were manufactured in a dull grey polyamide that looked very dowdy in comparison with the traditional Mercedes chrome trims with painted centres. The alternative was a new 16-hole alloy wheel, which would be made for Mercedes by wheel specialists Fuchs. This, too, was designed to have a flush face.

Less controversial, but equally revealing of the attention to aerodynamic detail that went into the W201, was the arrangement of the door mirrors. In typical Mercedes fashion, only the mirror on the driver's side was standard; the optional item on the passenger's side, when fitted, was different in shape. The designers had worked out that a smaller mirror would do all that was required on the passenger's side and would interfere less with the airflow. Despite the additional complication in terms of production, the W201 would always have 'lop-sided' mirrors – and the approach was later carried over to the W124 medium-sized saloons as well. Both mirrors could be adjusted from the inside, and it was again typical of Mercedes thinking that the passenger's side mirror was electrically adjusted while the one on the driver's side (which could be more easily reached) had to be adjusted by hand!

Along the flanks of the car, the only decoration was a slim rubber bump strip that, like so many elements in Mercedes designs, served two purposes. Most obviously, it helped to protect the doors against parking knocks, but it also had an impact on the appearance of the car, helping it to look longer and lower than it really was. Like the door mirrors, it was matt black. A similarly coloured plastic insert was used for the rain channels on the roof. This incorporated anchor points that could be used for a roof rack or a ski rack, and it also disguised the joins between the side pressings and the roof panel. The W201 had a 'monoside' design, where each body side was a single pressing and each major pressing was joined to the other by the roof and the floorpan.

As was expected on a Mercedes, the bonnet was arranged to lift to a convenient height for minor maintenance in the engine bay, while unhindered access could be achieved by releasing catches on the hinges, allowing it to be opened to 90 degrees from the horizontal. Similar thinking was evident in the design of the boot lid, which opened to a near-vertical position to give maximum access to the boot. A low loading sill was another welcome feature. Following the lead of the W126 S Class, the bumper aprons were made of polyurethane and were designed to spring back into shape after a low-speed impact. The material was self-coloured, and Sacco's team arranged for it to be available in either grey or beige to suit the paintwork of the car. It must be said that, although the grey always worked well, with some colours the beige did not.

The final shape of the W201 saloons was approved by the Mercedes board on 6 March 1979, several months before the W126 models introduced Bruno Sacco's new take on Mercedes styling at the Frankfurt motor show. There would of course be some further work for special derivatives – notably the high-performance 190E 2.3-16 – and there would be a facelift five years after the W201 had entered production, but the basic shape remained unchanged for the full ten-year life of the car.

Of course, Stuttgart's designers and engineers, being as enthusiastic and innovative as those of other companies, were unable to resist the temptation to develop ideas for derivatives that did not enter production. Over the next few years, there would be some design studies for a roadster

MERCEDES PROJECT CODES

Mercedes had a well-established system of project codes by the time it started work on the W201 compact saloons.

New car projects were allocated a code beginning with W, which stood for *Wagen* (German for 'car'). This was followed by a three-digit number, apparently chosen largely at random. Nevertheless, runs of numbers were sometimes used for related models. The codes W114 and W115 were allocated respectively to the six-cylinder and four-cylinder variants of a common design, the so-called 'Strich 8' (Stroke 8) medium-sized saloons introduced in 1968. The W201's successor was known as the W202, and that car's successor was a W203; all the numbers up to and including W206 have been allocated to successive generations of the compact Mercedes saloons.

Engine codes always began with M (for *Motor*, always petrol-powered) or OM (for *Ölmotor*, or diesel engine). These also typically had a three-digit identifying number. These numbers might also attract a suffix to indicate a variant (*see Appendix II*): so an M102 E 18 would be a 1.8-litre M102 engine with fuel injection (E for *Einspritzung* or 'injection'), while an M102 V 20 was a 2.0-litre M102 engine with a carburettor (V for *Vergaser*, or 'carburettor').

derivative, but this did not progress far and in fact a compact roadster would not join the Mercedes range until the R170 SLK model was announced in 1996. There would also be some serious thoughts about a two-door cabriolet derivative (*see* Chapter 5).

STRUCTURE AND SAFETY

Bruno Sacco's stylists worked closely with the body engineers at Mercedes to ensure that the new design could realistically be manufactured in quantity, met all the company's traditional safety standards (which were stricter than many mandated by government regulations around the world at the time), and was as light as practicable in order to minimize fuel consumption.

The bodyshell was designed so that there would be no significant intrusion into the passenger compartment in Mercedes' standard crash test, which involved a 40 per cent overlap front-end collision at 55km/h (34mph). There was no separate chassis, of course, but the chassis-like side members at the front of the car below the engine bay were designed to crumple progressively, and were forked at their rear ends to spread the collision forces. Around the passenger cabin was an inner structure of beams and cross-members arranged to resist the forces of an impact.

At the rear, the bodyshell was again arranged to crumple progressively in the event of an impact. The fuel tank was located behind the rear seat and above the suspension, as far out of harm's way as possible, and the spare wheel mounted below the boot floor was also intended to help absorb the forces of a rear-end impact.

The Mercedes engineers had to make sure that the

The boot of the W201 could not be as long from front to rear as on the larger cars, so it was made deep instead.

View of the construction of the roof: careful detail design of the structure ensured that the W201 offered crash safety at least equal to that of its larger siblings.

W201's bodyshell was as strong as those of the model's larger siblings, in order to meet the impact deformation requirements. In order to save weight, they made use of several ultra-modern materials, some of which had rarely been seen in the motor industry at that stage. In areas where strength was less critical, they specified aluminium and polycarbonates, and for 16 per cent of the steel structure they used HSLA (High-Strength, Low-Alloy) steel that allowed thinner and therefore lighter metalwork. With an eye to longevity, they also made use of a significant quantity of galvanized steel in the bodyshell to resist corrosion.

Mercedes had always maintained that there were two elements in safety design: active safety and passive safety. The passive elements were those that minimized injuries in an accident, such as the design of the bodyshell. The active elements were those that were designed to prevent an accident in the first place, and included items such as brakes and steering, which gave the driver maximum control at all times.

Crash tests in pilot-production examples confirmed the safety aspects of the W201 design.

The second crash test was designed to see how the rear of the car behaved under impact. Note that both crash-test cars have the number 82 on the side, which indicates the year of the test (1982).

Active safety was also served by the driver's ability to see clearly. To that end, the W201 was designed with a new type of windscreen wiper that was a 'first' for the company and would later be adopted for the 124-series medium-sized cars. Instead of the traditional pair of wiper arms, Mercedes drew up a single arm for the W201. The idea was not entirely new – the Citroën CX had used just such a design on its introduction in 1974, at least partly for aerodynamic reasons. The single arm pivoted from just below the centre of the windscreen and carried twin blades, one at the pivot end and one at the free end. It all worked very efficiently, but when it was released for production the wiper swept only 75 per cent of the windscreen as compared to the 78 per cent swept by the traditional twin wipers on the 123-series Mercedes. Clearly, further design work was needed. When a revised single-arm system was released in January 1985, it had been made to sweep no less than 86 per cent of the screen area.

SUSPENSION, STEERING AND BRAKES

There was more innovation in the design of the W201's suspension, which was drawn up both to minimize the space needed and to give this lighter and smaller car a ride quality that would be comparable to that of a W126 S Class. The design adopted was also very effective at reducing the transmission of road noise into the passenger cabin. In addition, it offered good handling, with much better roadholding than, for example, the contemporary BMW 3 Series (one of the target rival models), which was notorious for a sudden transition to tail-out oversteer on wet roads.

Suspension design was in fact one of the first areas on which Stuttgart's engineers focused; the light weight of the planned compact saloon meant that it would not behave like existing Mercedes and that in turn meant that existing designs might prove inadequate. In order to test a variety of ideas in

Various suspension configurations were
tested on the skeleton-like test rig.

The test rig still survives, but now wears
W201 wheel trims, which of course it could
not have had when it was first used.

Cutaway model showing the layout of
the front suspension, with the damper
struts and spring located separately.

The model also shows the location of the front anti-
roll bar. The brakes were discs on all four wheels.

the shortest possible time, the engineers built a driveable test rig on which the front and rear suspensions could easily be swapped. This was in use by autumn 1978. Mercedes later claimed that a total of seventy-seven different suspension designs had been drawn up, of which twenty-three were actually tested.

The most effective design of front suspension had a single wishbone and a strut, but this was not a conventional Ford-style MacPherson strut layout. Instead, the spring and damper were mounted separately, which had the advantage of reducing the height needed and of leaving more room in the engine compartment. The layout also reduced nose-dive under braking and the damper was able to react better than in a MacPherson strut because it was located closer to the wheel. The Mercedes design used a new gas damper, developed in conjunction with specialists Fichtel und Sachs at Schweinfurt. It was of course supplemented by an anti-roll bar.

Eight different rear suspension layouts were tried on that test rig, ranging from a De Dion type through to Mercedes' beloved (and traditional) swing-axles. In the end, the suspension engineers realized that they needed to come up with a completely new design for the W201. The one they eventually settled on was a multi-link system, which brought advantages of space and weight. A broadly similar system had been tried on one of the CIII experimental cars, but the W201's system was designed specifically for the car and was quite significantly different.

The innovative design adopted for production was a five-link type. Not only was it some 25–30 per cent lighter than the swing-axle rear suspension on the 123-series models, it also gave better ride and handling. Its layout is best understood from an illustration, but it can be explained as having a top wishbone that consisted of two separate links, a bottom wishbone that also consisted of two separate links, and a camber control arm located just below the wheel centre. Careful angling of the links gave excellent control of wheel movement by preventing both excessive camber change and changes of attitude under acceleration or braking. All the

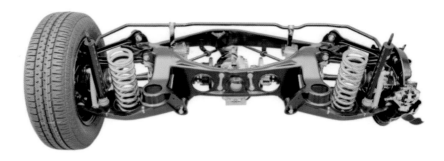

The differential and the rear suspension were carried on a sub-frame that bolted to the body.

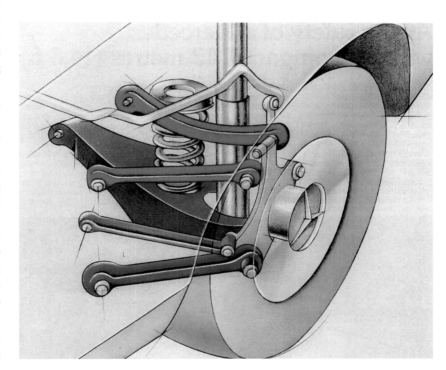

The layout of the five-link rear suspension gave the compact Mercedes a ride quality that was as good as that of an S Class, with excellent handling as well.

links were light in weight, being pressed from steel, and all were joined to a forged-steel upright that carried the wheel hub. The whole of the rear suspension was carried on a light sub-frame that also carried the final drive and was flexibly mounted to the underside of the bodyshell, and an anti-roll bar was made standard.

Steering was also carefully considered during the development stage. Although there would have been room for a sharp and direct rack-and-pinion system, the Mercedes engineers chose to stick with their tried-and-tested recirculating-ball type. Their primary reasons were that this was less prone to kickback than a rack-and-pinion system and that it was easier to adapt to minimize rearward movement of the steering column in a collision. As adopted for production, the column was designed to telescope under impact and to deflect downwards about the coupling between the column and the steering box. A power-assisted option was also developed, which required three turns of the wheel between locks and felt a lot sportier in use than the unassisted type with five turns from lock to lock. Unsurprisingly, the power-assisted system became the popular choice and would in fact be standardized in September 1985.

All-round disc brakes were only to be expected; they were already in production on the 123-series medium-sized cars as well as the larger Mercedes and the sports models. Floating-caliper types were chosen for the front wheels, with the aim of reducing heat transfer to the discs. The handbrake was arranged to act on separate drums within the rear discs, and a vacuum servo was chosen as standard equipment. The twin hydraulic circuits were split between front and rear, in the usual Mercedes fashion, and, although the brake pipes were made of corrodible steel, they were covered in plastic for protection and to resist corrosion. Of course, an ABS system was also designed, although in the beginning it would not be standard but would be made available as an expensive option.

MERCEDES FACTORIES

Mercedes-Benz passenger cars were made by a division of the Daimler-Benz company, which had been established in 1926 when the two leading car companies in Germany merged for mutual benefit. The company had always had its headquarters at Stuttgart in southern Germany, but over the years it had also opened several factories in other parts of Germany, as well as overseas.

The design headquarters, the body plant and the main car assembly lines were located in Sindelfingen, a small city some 15km from Stuttgart. Production of engines, transmissions and axles was the responsibility of a second factory at Untertürkheim, in the outer suburbs of Stuttgart, although this was supported by some other smaller plants in the same region. Also at Untertürkheim was the research and development division, which had its own banked test track.

A third factory – at Bremen – would become important in the W201 story. It had once been the Borgward factory, but under Daimler-Benz ownership had been developed to build light commercial vehicles. From 1978, it also assembled the estate variants of the medium-sized 123-series cars, and in 1984 it became a second assembly plant for the W201s alongside Sindelfingen. The two factories also shared W201 body production in an innovative arrangement that is explained in more detail in Chapter 2.

ENGINES

Once the decision had been made to use rear-wheel drive for the W201, there was no need to think about designing a transverse engine of the type usually associated with front-wheel drive. There was also a fairly obvious choice for the petrol engine option. Under development in the late 1970s was a new four-cylinder engine known as the M102 type. Initially intended to replace the older four-cylinder engines in the 123-series models, it was designed to provide engines of between 2.0 litres and 2.5 litres and was introduced in the 123-series models at the Frankfurt motor show in 1979.

Central to the design brief for the M102 engines was a reduction in both weight and physical size in comparison with the engines they replaced. This was achieved by using computer-aided design techniques that were quite new at the time. The engines were also drawn up to share as many common features as possible with a new six-cylinder that was called the M103. Both would have a single-overhead-camshaft design, with cast-iron cylinder blocks for durability and to minimize noise transmission. Their cylinder heads would be made of aluminium alloy, with a cross-flow design and hemispherical combustion chambers, and the camshaft would be driven conventionally by a single-row roller chain. A viscous-coupled fan minimized power wastage, while service intervals were extended to 12,000 miles to help reduce maintenance costs.

Maximum flexibility was another important factor in the design. Apart from variations in bore and stroke, the aim was to achieve different power outputs through carburettor and injected variants. The first production variants of these engines were to be a carburettor 2.0-litre (for the 123-series 200 model) and an injected 2.3-litre (for the

The existing M102 2.0-litre petrol engine was chosen for entry-level models, and would be fitted with a Stromberg carburettor.

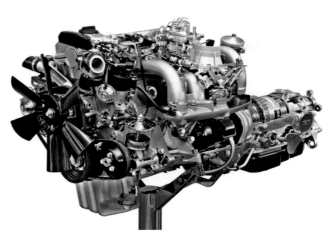

For the quicker and more expensive 190E model, the 2.0-litre M102 engine was equipped with Bosch fuel injection.

Mercedes loved demonstration cutaways; this one shows the injected 2.0-litre engine.

The Bosch injection pump on the cutaway 2.0-litre engine.

123-series 230E). Further-developed versions of these engines would also be used for the W201, and it is very likely that the engines team under Dr Hans-Otto Derndinger also investigated smaller-capacity types for the W201. They were certainly feasible – a 1.8-litre M102 variant did go into production in 1990.

The choice for the first W201s eventually came down to three variants of this engine. Entry-level models would have a carburettor 2.0-litre, somewhat detuned from its 123-series 200 form. Above this in the W201 hierarchy would be an injected 2.0-litre unit. In addition, to compensate for the power-sapping effects of the emissions-control equipment required in the USA, cars for that market would have an injected 2.3-litre engine.

All Mercedes models by this stage had a diesel engine option and the W201 would be no exception. Once again, there was a fairly obvious choice because work had begun in late 1977 on a new range of modular diesel engines for passenger cars. The smallest of these was a four-cylinder called the OM601, which would have a 2.0-litre capacity and would deliver (just) enough power and torque to give the diesel W201 the sort of performance that its likely buyers would expect. For the USA, where a diesel option would meet expectations of any new Mercedes, emissions-control equipment would again reduce engine power, so a larger-capacity, 2.2-litre version of the engine was designed. It would only ever be used in the W201 range and, like the 2.0-litre diesel in models for other countries, it would not be introduced until the petrol-engined cars had been on sale for a year.

The design parameters for both the M102 petrol and OM601 diesel engines had been established before the shape of the W201 saloons had been settled. This created a minor problem in that both engines were too tall to fit under the compact saloon's low bonnet. As a result, both would be installed with a 15-degree tilt to the right. The Stromberg carburettor of the petrol engine also had to be reduced in height to fit.

GEARBOXES

A five-speed manual gearbox was an option in the 123-series cars after 1980, but the standard type had four speeds. It was this version that the Mercedes engineers chose to use in the W201 as well. A five-speed would certainly have given better fuel economy (and a new one was indeed designed as

an option for the W201), but the extra cost counted against it: it was important to keep the compact saloon's showroom price down if it was to be perceived as a new and more affordable Mercedes-Benz.

As an alternative, there would be a four-speed automatic, newly designed for the W201 but soon to be made available in other models as well. The W4A 020 gearbox was a further development of the existing Mercedes-built automatic, with modifications to reduce internal power losses and to achieve a lower weight. Like other Mercedes automatic gearboxes (and unlike most other makes), it had a secondary oil pump that made it tolerant of tow-starting the car and of suspended towing without first unbolting the propellor shaft. It also automatically selected second gear at idle in order to reduce 'creep', but would kick down to first for a rapid getaway.

Axle gearing for the W201s was chosen to give good economy. Top speeds were quite reasonable, although the automatic gearbox would make both the diesel and the carburettor petrol models tediously slow to drive.

INTERIOR

The design of the interior presented a major challenge, because the reduced dimensions of the passenger cabin meant that compromises had to be found. Bruno Sacco's team chose to design the front of the compartment as much like an existing Mercedes as possible, and to make the space sacrifices in the rear.

Even so, the dashboard was completely redesigned, with a new and sweeping form in place of the elegant curves of existing models. The existing Mercedes instrument layout was widely admired and there was no reason not to retain it. As a result, the overall appearance was recognizably Mercedes, but updated and streamlined. The three-dial layout featured a speedometer in the centre, three smaller gauges in segments on the left, and a clock on the right. To appeal to those who wanted a sportier layout, the designers came up with a rev counter that incorporated a small time clock and could replace the standard right-hand dial. There was a row of warning lights along the bottom of the instrument cluster.

As on the 123-series cars, a single multi-function stalk on the column covered the functions that were usually assigned to at least two stalks. Despite repeated concerns in the motoring press (especially the British magazines) that it was 'overloaded', the system actually worked extremely well.

The rotary heater controls below the main dashboard were also very similar to those on the 123-series models, although the controls for air volume and direction swapped sides. The whole design reflected the Mercedes ideal of functional simplicity.

There were some compromises, of course. The steering wheel was large by contemporary standards (even though it was actually a centimetre smaller in diameter than its equivalent on the 123 models) and thigh room for the driver was reduced. Mercedes was nevertheless wedded to a large steering wheel, to give the necessary control, so the designers had little scope for change. The glovebox was very small – too small, in fact, to hold the vehicle handbook.

Front space was generally good, even though the cabin was narrower than that of other Mercedes models. In the rear it was less comfortable. Although legroom was better than that in a BMW 3 Series, it was disappointing to those used to older Mercedes models. The front seats were designed with plenty of adjustment; in fact, it was possible to move them back so far that rear seat legroom almost ceased to exist. This was another compromise that the designers had to accept. The narrow cabin and footwells also made it impossible to give the W201 a foot-operated parking brake, such as that used on all new Mercedes designs since 1968. Instead, the designers provided a conventional handbrake between the front seats.

Upholstery was largely dictated by existing Mercedes

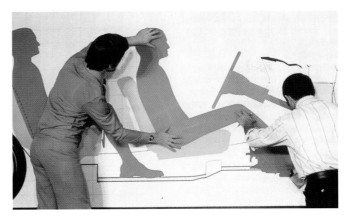

The picture was probably posed for the camera, but it demonstrates how the designers worked on the seating layout by using full-size two-dimensional drawings.

standards. There seemed no reason to downgrade it, so MB-Tex grained vinyl was standard, with cloth and velour options; leather was also offered, although in practice it would not become available until January 1984.

There was a slight miscalculation by the designers (or their overlords) in one area: the W201 was introduced with a remarkably sombre and uninspiring selection of interior colour options, most of which were at variance with the expectations of the under-30-year-olds at whom the W201 was aimed.

With the centre pillar removed from this demonstration cutaway, the layout of the passenger cabin can be seen. Priority was given to space for the front-seat passengers.

A MISLEADING PROTOTYPE

Mounting press speculation about the forthcoming new compact Mercedes was fuelled by some scoop photographs of a small hatchback model, which were published in the German *Auto Zeitung* of 20 July 1981. Taken by the well-known 'spy' photographer Hans G Lehmann, they showed what appeared to be a small front-engined hatchback that was about the size of a VW Golf. When they were unable to gain any helpful insights from the Mercedes press office, the *Auto Zeitung* editorial team allowed imagination to run riot.

They got it wrong, of course, and the truth about this car did not emerge until 2012, when Mercedes released some pictures and information to the media on the occasion of the W201's 30th anniversary. In essence, the 1981 car had been a 'mule' prototype, based on a W201 and intended to test ideas for an eventual small city car. That appeared in concept form as the NAFA (*Nahverkehrsfahrzeug*, or 'short-distance car') during 1981 and was really a distant ancestor of the A Class Mercedes that was prototyped in 1996.

The hatchback prototype was essentially a cut-and-shut W201, with only two seats (like the NAFA) but a decent-sized boot and a hatchback design that used the cut-down tailgate of a 123-series estate car. Just 3,515mm long, it had a wheelbase of around 2,250mm and weighed 1,060kg. It was powered by an injected M102 2.0-litre engine (as would be used in the 190E) and the rear wheels were driven through a five-speed gearbox.

The little hatchback prototype based on a 190E that caused excitement in the German press ...

... and its successors: the NAFA prototype in the foreground and the production A Class at the back.

The front end was of course made to look anonymous, and – partly for disguise and partly for convenience – the door handles were taken from a Mk I VW Golf. When the car went out on the road, it wore a Cologne licence plate and Ford hub caps, which would have suggested to curious onlookers that it was a prototype from the German branch of the Ford empire. By the time it was shown to the press, however, it was wearing W201-style alloy wheels; no doubt Mercedes thought it tactful not to upset their counterparts at Ford by using the original configuration!

PROTOTYPES

Early mechanical development of the W201 was carried out in the usual way on 'mule' prototypes. Some of these were existing production Mercedes cars modified with elements of the proposed new model. Others had experimental running-gear in what have been described as 'stretched' VW Golf bodies. Some of the early ones, built in 1978, had front-wheel drive.

The first full prototypes, with the production body design, were built in 1980. Track testing at Untertürkheim was followed by testing both in Germany and abroad, especially in Finland, where the behaviour of the cars in ultra-cold conditions could be monitored. The prototypes that left Stuttgart were registered in Aachen (which issues numbers prefixed with an A) rather than in Stuttgart (which uses an S), in order to put onlookers off the scent. They were also disguised with bland-looking front and rear sheet metal, and some wore Ushido badges, to suggest a Japanese origin.

Even so, it was not long before press photographers recognized them for what they were and scoop pictures began to appear in print. Perhaps the designers at Stuttgart should have been flattered because, despite their disguise, the W201s were quite readily recognizable as Mercedes products! Incorporating all the lessons learned from the test cars, the first W201s were hand-built to production standard in autumn 1981. Of course, there was by this stage intense press interest in them when they were spotted. Pilot production followed in February 1982 and volume production began – slowly at first – that October.

Between January 1974 and January 1982, Mercedes spent an estimated £600 million developing the new W201 models and on equipping its factories to build them. It was a huge gamble but, thanks to its usual meticulous planning, the company was quietly confident. And its confidence was not misplaced. Despite a slightly hesitant start to sales when the compact saloon reached showrooms at the end of 1982, it would go on to become a strong seller and to establish the company firmly in a new sector of the market.

An early prototype pictured during cold-weather testing in the Arctic. The disguise was quite effective, even though it is clear with hindsight that this was a Mercedes W201!

THE NAME

Just one thing remained to be established when the engineers had finished their work: what should the new model be called? Traditionally, Mercedes cars were known by a number that indicated their engine size, so, for example, a car with a 2.5-litre engine was a 250. Suffix letters were sometimes added to avoid confusion when the same engine appeared in different models, so a 250 was different from a 250SE or a 250SL.

The entry-level models of the existing medium-size range were the 200 and 200D, the latter with a diesel engine. The W201 was to share its 2-litre petrol engine with the 123-series cars, which further complicated the naming issue. Finding a suffix that would mark out the W201 as a smaller car than the 123-series was not easy. The Mercedes marketing people decided that the car should be called a 190 and that was how the public would know it from then on.

Later prototypes were less well disguised, although several details on these cars would have misled anybody who saw them at the time.

CHAPTER TWO

THE FIRST THREE YEARS, 1982–1985

Mercedes' new compact saloons were introduced to the world's media at an event in Andalusia, southern Spain, on 8 December 1982. While the representatives of the press were trying out the new cars, the first examples were being delivered to Mercedes dealers and the car went on sale the very next day, on 9 December.

FIRST PETROL MODELS

At the beginning, just two models were available: the carburettor-fed 190 and the injected 190E. Both were powered by variants of the same M102 2.0-litre petrol engine and, unusually for Mercedes, no diesel model was announced. One was certainly in the pipeline, but restrictions on factory space (*see below*) were a key reason why it was initially held over. Both the 190 and the 190E came as standard with a four-speed manual gearbox, but a four-speed automatic was also available at extra cost.

Engine

The M102.921 engine in the 190 models delivered just 90PS.

The round air cleaner marks this out as a carburettor 190 engine. Note how an additional bulkhead protected items such as the battery, wiper motor and fuse box.

The W201 was a very neat design. It was rather modern-looking for the
time, despite the traditional big Mercedes radiator grille.

Right-hand-drive models were released a few months after production had begun. The sleek, sculpted lines of this 190E are very apparent, and the badges on the tail are in the typically discreet but quite unmistakeable Mercedes style.

BELOW: **A larger air cleaner was used for the injected engine of the 190E. The layout of the engine bay is otherwise very similar indeed to that of the entry-level 190.**

It was closely related to the 109PS M102 engine of the same capacity in the 123-series 200 models, but had smaller ports and valves and a lower valve lift, which restricted its power. For some export markets, there was also an 86PS version that was designed to run on low-octane petrol. Both versions of the engine were slightly lighter in weight than their 123-series counterparts, as the Mercedes engineers had managed to shave 8kg (more than 17lb) off by a series of small modifications.

Obviously, one reason for the lower power in the 190 engine was marketing: there had to be a clear specification distinction between the compact and the medium-sized saloons. However, there were other important reasons. With the more powerful version of the engine, the 190 would have been able to exceed 180km/h (112mph) and would therefore have needed more expensive HR-rated tyres. It would also have been more expensive to insure. By limiting its power and performance, Mercedes was reinforcing the point that this new model was less expensive to buy and to own than those that had gone before it.

In the 190E, the engine was an M102.962 type that produced 122PS. It was not the first injected version of the M102 – the 2.3-litre type in the 123-series 230E had an all-mechanical K-Jetronic injection system – but it was the first Mercedes engine to use the KE-Jetronic. This was a low-pressure system that combined features of the K-Jetronic with some from the all-electronic L-Jetronic type; its main functions were mechanical, but electronic controls were used to cut fuel on the over-run, to deal with cold-start enrichment, and at full power.

Crucially, the KE-Jetronic would still allow the engine to run if the electronic system failed. When functioning correctly, it allowed economy gains of up to 30 per cent in a cold engine, and the electronic side of the system also provided an easier means of controlling the mixture through a Lambda probe to meet emissions-control regulations. This was not needed yet in the 2.0-litre engine, but it certainly would be needed in the 2.3-litre type that was being prepared for the USA.

Gearbox

The manual gearbox in both cars was essentially the same as the one in the 123-series models, but it had shed weight as part of the programme to make the W201 as light as possible. By contrast, the W4A 020 automatic gearbox had been drawn up specifically for the compact range, and it weighed 8kg (17.6lb) less than its equivalent in the 123 models. It had been designed using the principles established for Mercedes' existing automatic gearboxes, but the designers had achieved reductions in both internal friction and torque converter slip. On the over-run, the gearbox would normally change down into second gear, which minimized the uncontrolled freewheeling associated with many automatic gearboxes; under acceleration, it also changed up quickly into top gear, to improve fuel economy. Older automatics had typically increased fuel consumption by around 10 per cent as compared with their manual equivalents, but for this one Mercedes claimed that manual and automatic gearboxes gave directly comparable economy.

Production and Reactions

Production volumes began in late 1982 at 110 cars a day, but this was quickly ramped up to 438 a day during 1983. By 1984, W201 production was running at 890 cars a day, although there was a slight reduction to 857 a day when the new mid-range W124 models entered production to replace the old W123 types. Before production had begun, Mercedes had predicted that 30 per cent of W201s would go to customers who were new to the marque, but early returns from the German market suggested that the proportion was more like 50 per cent. This was success indeed. The car was also proving a strong seller outside Germany, and the 35 per cent of production that had been exported in 1982–1983 increased to 44 per cent for 1984 and 1985. The company had hoped to make 4,000 cars in 1982 and to build 100,000 in 1983, but they did better than that. The build total for 1982 was actually 4,650 and that for 1983 was 109,837.

All seemed well and the response to the new models was generally favourable. There were, inevitably, a few doubters who considered that the car was not a proper Mercedes, but the company was prepared to take such criticism in its stride. The biggest concern, perhaps, was the rather negative reaction to the pricing. Customers expected the new small Mercedes to be quite a lot cheaper than the mid-range cars, when in fact it was priced only a little below them. In such circumstances, the fact that a lock for the glovebox was an extra-cost option on all models seemed to be unnecessary penny-pinching.

An early car showing the standard configuration with only a driver's door mirror. From this angle, the family resemblance to other Mercedes models of the time was very obvious.

The passenger door mirror, when fitted, was smaller than the one that was standard on the driver's side. This one is on a right-hand-drive car.

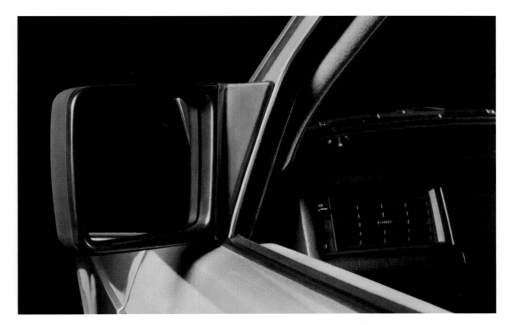

BELOW: The three-dial layout in front of the driver was beautifully clear, as always, but in the W201 it was mounted within the dashboard rather than as a separate unit.

Press Reaction

The factory claimed a top speed of 175km/h (108.7mph) for the carburettor 190, which was a little on the conservative side. The German magazine *mot* recorded 181.4km/h (112.7mph) on test. From rest to 100km/h took a rather disappointing 14.2 seconds. The injected car was of course far more sprightly. Mercedes claimed a 195km/h (121mph) maximum, which as usual was conservative; some magazine tests reported a top speed of 200km/h (124.2mph). *Auto Zeitung* in Germany saw 197km/h (122.4mph) in a manual-gearbox car and 10.5 seconds for the 0–100km/h sprint. *Auto, Motor und Sport* tested an automatic 190E and reported 193km/h (120mph) with a 0–100km/h time of 11.8 seconds. This was a quick car for its time and especially for its class.

In Britain, the car was not released until September 1983, by which time Mercedes had made a number of changes to the original specification. Understandably, press interest also focused on the 190E rather than the carburettor 190. Nevertheless, *Autocar* of 11 December 1982 did record some impressions of an early car. 'It's a lively car to drive,' wrote Michael Scarlett, 'in a way that no 200 ever was. It sounds lively, too, when pushed, the engine noise not being particularly well suppressed, although it's a pleasing sort of sound which won't annoy.' He found no vices in the handling and praised its comfort, although he did have one serious reservation, which was that rear-seat legroom was poor compared with some rivals in the 2.0-litre class.

The AA's *Drive* magazine was able to try one of the very first right-hand-drive 190E models to reach Britain for its December 1983 issue. This had an automatic gearbox, but was early enough not to have the switchable modes that became standard in November 1984. It was, the magazine reported, 'still every inch a Mercedes', but the journalist 'felt that £10,640 was a lot of money for a car without alloy wheels, electric windows, radio/tape cassette player, and so on…. Mind you, if you can afford it you won't be disappointed.' (In practice, the test car had several options that increased its showroom cost to £16,143; in that, it was not untypical of a lot of 190E models in the real world.)

An over-reading speedometer was a minor annoyance and, in the wet, 'the amount of rear-end grip did give… some cause for concern'. As for the suspension, it was 'super at soaking-up high-speed problems', but it could be 'caught out by the slower ones'. There was a lack of 'feel' in the power-assisted steering, but the car was quick enough, with a 114mph top speed (Mercedes claimed 118mph) and

Two very early UK-market models, then in use by MBUK staff, conveniently parked together at an event. Both colours – Orient Red and Classic White – would be discontinued for 1985. Side repeater indicators had not yet become a standard UK-market feature.

Early UK-market cars did not have the selectable Sport and Economy modes for their automatic gearbox. The switches around the gear lever show that this one has several extras: electric windows all round, a rear radio speaker (plus the latest Becker Grand Prix electronic radio-cassette head unit), and heated seats. The seats are also upholstered in the optional leather.

The standard dashboard had a large clock in the right-hand position, but this could be replaced by a rev counter with a small inset clock. This is on a right-hand-drive car. Interestingly, Mercedes did not swap the positions of the two outer dials so that the clock could be seen by rear-seat passengers – which it could on left-hand-drive cars.

a 0–60mph time of 10.6 seconds. The reporter went on to observe that, 'with the accelerator floored, the engine note [became] a purposeful bark', and a 'gentle cruise across Europe returned a remarkable consumption of a true 30.2mpg'. However, he considered that he would be 'very unlikely to match that figure driving round at home, where the opportunities for sustained speeds are very remote'.

MAKING SPACE

Factory space at Mercedes' Sindelfingen plant in Stuttgart had been tight for many years. Volumes for the new compact saloon were anticipated to be high and, from early in the W201 project, the company had recognized that it would have insufficient room to build the cars. The original plan was therefore to install the assembly lines for the W201s at the Bremen assembly plant.

The Bremen factory, in the Sebaldsbrück suburb of the city, had been opened in 1938 by the old Borgward company and in the later 1950s had turned out that company's highly regarded Isabella models. When Borgward folded, in 1961, the factory passed to Rheinstahl-Hanomag, which was succeeded in 1969 by Hanomag-Henschel. In 1970, Daimler-

Benz acquired this company and with it the Bremen factory. By the end of the 1970s, it was turning out light commercial vehicles and also the estate variants of the medium-sized 123-series saloons.

However, the plan to build the W201s at Bremen ran into trouble when both the trades unions and the local council raised objections. Although these difficulties were eventually resolved, they dragged on long enough to make it impossible for the Bremen factory to be ready in time for the planned launch of the W201 at the end of 1982. Mercedes had to settle for a compromise. The new assembly lines were installed at Sindelfingen in the knowledge that they would have a limited capacity of 140,000 units per year. This would be good enough for the first year and then production could be expanded when the Bremen plant came on stream.

Bremen was eventually ready in the late summer of 1983, when it assembled pilot-production examples of the models it was to build. However, it was the Sindelfingen plant that celebrated completion of the 100,000th W201 (a 190E) on 22 November of that year. Once both plants were fully operational, their combined maximum production capacity for the W201 models was 300,000 cars a year. It was a total that left plenty of room for expansion; despite strong demand for the model, the highest annual total actually achieved was 211,804 for the 1985 calendar-year.

Mercedes made significant use of robots on the W201 assembly lines, both
to ensure consistency and to reduce production times.

The production lines, initially only at Sindelfingen, began turning out W201s in late 1982. The bonnets are raised to 90 degrees here to allow the engines to be installed.

The balance of production would gradually change in favour of Bremen, which built only a third of all W201s in 1984 but was up to 55 per cent for 1985. Nevertheless, there were some teething troubles while the plant worked up to capacity. During the first year of production, for example, Mercedes recalled 13,000 cars for faults associated with the handbrake or the rear dampers; this was at a time when recalls for Mercedes products were almost unheard of.

A complicated production-sharing system had been worked out to make the best use of the capacity available at both assembly plants. The Bremen factory made the floor assemblies, fuel tanks, bonnets and doors for both plants, shipping quantities to the Sindelfingen assembly lines several hundred miles away. At Sindelfingen, meanwhile, all the other sheet-metal components were produced, and appropriate quantities were shipped to Bremen for the assembly lines there. Meanwhile, both assembly plants were supplied with engines, transmissions and axles from the Stuttgart-Untertürkheim factory, and the Mercedes plant at Düsseldorf provided steering gear assemblies. This was the first time that the company had run such a complicated logistics operation, but it would function successfully without any major hitches for the next ten years.

FIRST REVISIONS

With both the Sindelfingen and Bremen assembly lines now turning out W201 models, Mercedes was able to make its first set of revisions to the compact models. Some were minor changes that had been prompted by customer experience with the cars; some were additional options that added appeal to the range. There was also one completely new model in the shape of the diesel 190D. The 1984-model changes were announced at the Frankfurt motor show in September 1983, where Mercedes also introduced a new high-performance model called the 190E 2.3-16 (although it would be a year before customers could actually buy one). Right-hand-drive variants also became available, along with the first variants for the US market (see Chapter 6).

Customer feedback had prompted a small number of changes. Four of the early paint colours were dropped and the boot handle was reinforced after some had distorted in service. The thick central pillars had hindered sideways vision out of the car, so they were slimmed down a little. The door seals had also given trouble, making the car so airtight that the doors almost invariably had to be slammed shut.

A rather interesting combination on what was probably a pre-production car: there is no wood trim around the gear lever, but the gate pattern moulded into the grip shows that the optional five-speed gearbox is fitted. The two actually appeared at the same time in volume production.

It had also been noted that the lack of a drip rail allowed rainwater to fall from the roof on to the outer edges of the seats. As a result, the 1984 models had new door seals with a lip to channel rainwater away. On the inside of the central pillars, the upper belt mountings were also modified.

There were changes to the dashboard area, too. Customers had apparently found the finish too plain, so a Zebrano wood insert was added to the centre console around the gear lever. It did brighten things up a little and even added a touch of class, although to some eyes it smacked of tokenism. The lower dashboard on 1983 models had been available in only three colours, but the choice now expanded so that this area was matched to any of the seven interior colour options.

The four-speed manual gearbox remained unchanged, except that reverse was now synchronized to allow faster selection without graunching. There were also some valuable improvements to the automatic option. This now came with a sliding switch mounted alongside the selector gate that gave electronic control of two modes of operation. E mode improved economy, giving a second-gear start, earlier upchanges and delayed downchanges, while the alternative S mode was supposed to be 'standard', but soon became more familiarly known as Sport mode.

A new five-speed manual gearbox option had an overdrive fifth gear that helped to reduce fuel consumption and noise at higher speeds. Its raised second and third ratios also contributed to better fuel economy. There had been a Getrag five-speed option in the 123-series models since 1980, but the gearbox in the W201s was different. It was not only a substantial 27kg (59.5lb) lighter but also had a slicker change action.

The extra-cost options included a neat headlamp wash-wipe system.

The OM601 four-cylinder diesel engine was specially developed for the 190 models, and was the smallest in a new modular diesel range. Like the petrol engines, it was installed with a 15-degree tilt to the right.

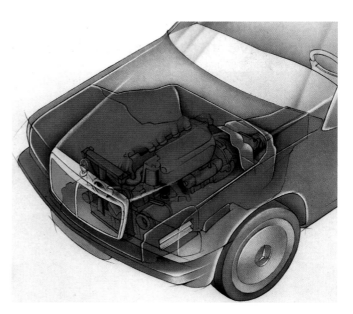

Mercedes illustrated the principles behind the noise encapsulation system like this. It would be used on later, larger-engined diesel W201s as well.

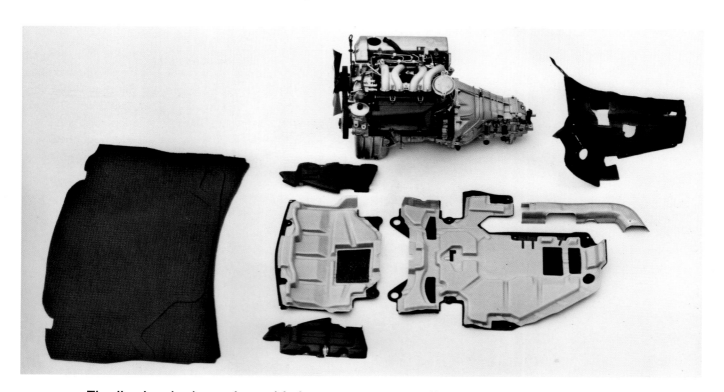

The diesel engine is seen here with the component parts of its noise encapsulation kit. On the left is the underbonnet pad; on the right are the sections that fitted below the engine and on the inner wings; and top right is insulation for the front of the transmission tunnel.

Also new on the options list were some stylish alloy wheels, which had the same 14-inch diameter and 5-inch rim as the standard steel type. These 16-hole items were manufactured by Fuchs at Meinerzhagen and gave the W201 models a much more stylish appearance than the rather functional-looking standard wheels and trims. They were not without their problems, though. Some early examples developed fine cracks during testing at the Hockenheim race track and dealers subsequently had to change a number of sets free of charge on customers' cars. (For the record, the affected wheels carried date codes between 3583 and 4983.)

THE 190D: A DIESEL 201

There had to be a diesel version of the 190 sooner or later, and in September 1983 Mercedes met public expectations by announcing a 190D model at the Frankfurt motor show. In fact, the pilot batch of twenty-eight cars had been assembled at Sindelfingen as early as August 1982, but the new diesel engine was not yet in full production and so volume production did not actually begin until November 1983, the same month in which sales began. All the early cars came from Sindelfingen, but the Bremen plant was also geared up to build the 190D; it built 208 pilot-production models in November 1983 and began volume production in March 1984.

**The usual discreet boot-lid badge marks this left-hand-drive model out
as a 190D. It is wearing the optional alloy wheels.**

**A favourite Mercedes publicity shot, showing the driver of a 190D choosing the
direction sign for the diesel pumps at a fuel stop on the Autobahn.**

A New Engine

It was only to be expected that the 190D would parallel its
petrol counterparts in every way except for its engine. That
proved to be the case. Called the OM601, the new four-
cylinder diesel was the first of a planned modular family of
four-, five- and six-cylinder engines that would feature common design elements and a common bore and stroke. Earlier
Mercedes diesel car engines had usually shared design elements with their petrol-powered contemporaries, but for
the first time the OM601 was a standalone design. Lower
and shorter than the OM615 2.0-litre engine that was still
being used in the mid-size 123-series cars, it also weighed
considerably less; indeed, it was actually lighter than the

190E's 2.0-litre petrol engine. This in itself was an important step forward, because diesel engines had traditionally
been more robustly constructed and therefore heavier than
petrol types of the same swept volume.

Development of this new diesel engine began in autumn
1977 under Kurt Obländer, who was then head of the Mercedes car engine division. The target was to produce a range
of engines that were significantly lighter in weight, mark-
edly more economical in their use of fuel, and delivered
more power than the Mercedes diesels then in production.
The engines team experimented with three basic designs.
A direct-injection design gave good fuel economy but was
noisy. They also tried a swirl-chamber design and indirect
injection (which was then in use on production Mercedes

car diesels). Indirect injection gave less power than direct injection but was much less noisy, and it also put less strain on the con-rods. This appears to have been a decisive factor in its selection as the preferred type.

The OM601 was drawn up as the first of these new engines, with its four cylinders each displacing just under 500cc to give a swept volume of just under 2 litres. The sides of the cast-iron block extended 65mm below the centre-line of the crankshaft, which ran in five bearings and carried four counter-weights. Traditionally, Mercedes car diesels had also had cast-iron cylinder heads, but Obländer's team drew this one up with an alloy head. It was a 'first' for the company and it helped greatly in weight saving. More compact than the OM615 2-litre diesel then in production for the mid-size W123-series saloons, the production OM601 actually weighed 48.5kg (107lb) less, and was 11kg (24lb) lighter than a 190E petrol engine of similar size.

In common with earlier Mercedes diesels, the OM601 had a single overhead camshaft driven by a duplex chain; caution prevented the company from experimenting with a belt drive. However, the cross-flow cylinder head was unusual for a diesel engine. Hydraulic tappets helped to minimize valve-train noise and all filters were positioned in such a way as to allow easy access, to aid servicing. Unusually long inlet pipes (which from the outside looked like a bunch of bananas) boosted mid-range torque. Earlier Mercedes car diesels had used piston-type fuel pumps, and the engines team stayed here with a four-piston type made by Bosch, adding a powerful in-tank pump that simplified re-starting if the tank had been allowed to run dry. A single auxiliary belt saved weight and also avoided complication, and a new vacuum pump took care of requirements for the brake servo, headlamp adjustment and other optional items. This single-belt drive would later be adopted for the petrol engines as well.

If 72PS at 4,600rpm does not sound very exciting today, for 1983 it was a revelation. The older OM615 2-litre diesel engine in the 123 range managed 60PS at 4,400rpm, and that was in a car that was much heavier than the W201. The power-per-litre figure actually made Mercedes' new diesel engine among the most powerful in the world, which must have been a source of considerable pride at Stuttgart. A thermostatically controlled heating element in the main fuel line prevented fuel waxing at sub-zero temperatures, which would make starting difficult. Quick-start glow plugs were standard. As a result, this engine did not require the two batteries that were then the norm for diesel engines.

Instead, a single 72Ah type from Bosch was enough to give reliable starting under all conditions; this, of course, saved both cost and weight. The OM601 was installed with a three-point mounting, two of the mountings being hydraulic to help damp out the characteristic diesel vibration that was, of course, still present.

Not content to stop there, Mercedes also introduced the 190D with a three-piece sound insulation capsule around the engine. This was another world 'first' in a series-production car. The company had experimented earlier with such a system on diesel-engined models from the medium-sized 123 range and also on some of its light commercial vehicles. On the 190D, the encapsulation reduced noise by 5 decibels, which to the human ear sounds like half. For 1983, it was another revelation, although the characteristic thrum of the diesel engine could still be heard quite clearly inside the passenger cabin.

The sections of insulation consisted of foam on a self-supporting plastic backing, with holes for air entry and for wires and piping. The lower section took up almost the whole of the bottom of the engine compartment. This and the side sections were supplemented by sound-deadening on the underside of the bonnet and on the front of the transmission tunnel. A thermostatically controlled shutter on the left-hand section allowed heat to be discharged so that the engine compartment could not become excessively hot. On cars with air conditioning, this was matched by a second shutter on the opposite side. Servicing was not made more complicated by all this insulation, as the engine was fully accessible with the bonnet open and the oil filter could be reached from above.

Obviously, the 190D was never going to be a ball of fire with just 72PS, but then it had not been designed to deliver startling performance. Its purpose was to deliver much better fuel economy than its petrol equivalent, thus bringing Mercedes ownership within the grasp of customers who could not afford the running costs of a petrol model. When *Autocar* in Britain tried a five-speed 190D for its issue of 24 October 1984, its most important finding was probably a typical fuel consumption of very nearly 34mpg.

Press Reaction

The factory claimed a top speed of 160km/h (99.4mph) for the 190D. When the Swiss *Automobil Revue* magazine tested one, it recorded a maximum of 163km/h (101.3mph), but *Autocar* in Britain achieved no more than 97mph. It took a long time to reach such speeds, of course; *Automobil Revue* said that the car took 17.5 seconds to reach 100km/h (62mph) from rest, while *Autocar* saw 60mph come up in 15.9 seconds. Few owners were probably tempted to achieve maximum speed anyway; much more important to most of them was the car's ability to cruise comfortably at 110–130km/h (roughly 70–80mph) on a motorway for hour after hour.

In Britain, where taxes on diesel fuel reduced its attraction in comparison with petrol, diesel cars were not popular, so it was unsurprising to find a very negative review in *Motor* magazine of 17 November 1984. 'Based on current fuel costs, the break-even point with running a diesel 190 compared with the petrol version will be 50,000 miles,' the magazine calculated, although it did acknowledge that 'servicing costs should be lower'. The five-speed 190D's performance came in for heavy criticism, too, with the test recording 17.7 seconds for the 0–60mph standing start, with a top speed of 99.4mph.

'The acceleration is poor to the point of embarrassment,' said *Motor*, describing it as 'far too sluggish for today's cut-and-thrust traffic conditions' and adding that 'unlike most diesels it does not pull very strongly'. The magazine also thought that 'the logic of spending over £10,000 on a car that can accelerate no quicker than a 1.0-litre Austin Metro must surely be questionable'. Nevertheless, the 'overall consumption figure of 34.6mpg is about 20 per cent better than what would be expected from a similar sized petrol-engined car'. The chassis was 'excellent', but the reviewer deemed it 'a shame' that 'the sophistication of its rear suspension is largely wasted with so little power at its disposal'.

THE 190E 2.3-16

Developing Performance

Mercedes-Benz had not been hugely successful in motorsport in the late 1970s, despite a serious programme focused on the 450SLC 5.0 coupé and the 280E and 280CE models. By 1980, the company was looking for a new opportunity that would bring success in the field and, with it, valuable publicity. The new compact W201 saloon looked as if it might provide the answer and the company for a time focused on developing it as a rally car to challenge the Ford Escorts and Talbot Lotus Sunbeams that were dominating the sport.

There would have to be a roadgoing version of the rally car as well, in order to meet the FISA homologation rules, so in September 1980 work began on a version of the W201 that the engineers called the Sport. The rally car and its roadgoing equivalent were not seen as a standalone project. The plan was to develop a four-valve version of one of the planned W201 production engines, which would not only bring extra performance but would also give Stuttgart more experience of the other benefits of four-valve configurations: improvements in fuel economy and reductions in exhaust emissions. Both factors were high on the Mercedes-Benz agenda at the time.

The decision was taken to sub-contract the design and development of this new engine to Cosworth Engineering. Based at Northampton in the UK, this company had been a world leader in four-valve engineering since 1966, earning enduring fame through its Ford Cosworth DFV racing engine. It had just branched out into consultancy work, making its expertise available to motor manufacturers generally. Cosworth had also developed a new thin-wall aluminium casting process known as Coscast, and would be able to produce the special cylinder heads on Mercedes' behalf at its new foundry in Worcester. For a model that was intended to have a limited production run (Mercedes planned to make just enough to meet the homologation requirements, and no more), this was an ideal arrangement. The decision was soon made that the base of the new engine should be the largest-capacity petrol engine that was destined at the time for the W201 range – the 2.3-litre four-cylinder M102 type.

However, the original plan to build a rally car was cancelled before it had really got off the ground. Just as it had been taking shape at Stuttgart, Audi announced its new Quattro model at the 1980 Geneva motor show. With four-wheel drive and a turbocharged engine delivering 200PS, this was a natural for the World Rally Championship that Mercedes had in mind. Even though it was not entered in serious competition until January 1981 (when it won the Jänner Rally in Austria), early demonstrations made clear that it would change the face of rallying. It was equally obvious that the planned W201 rally car would be completely outclassed. At the end of 1980, Mercedes formally withdrew from participation in rallies; it was probably at this stage that the plan for a rallying W201 was also abandoned.

Nevertheless, the idea of developing a four-valve W201 seems to have been firmly entrenched by this stage, not least because Stuttgart management did not want to leave the field clear for aftermarket tuning specialists to develop such an engine. Somebody saved the day by suggesting that the W201 Sport project could be re-focused to deliver a car that would be competitive in a different branch of motorsport – touring car racing.

The idea gained management support. Even if Mercedes had no plans to field a 'works' team, a high-performance W201 might well attract privateers, and any success on their part would bring positive publicity for the range as a whole. From this point on, the engineers began to think in terms of a Group A touring car challenger. The inauguration in 1984 of what became the DTM (Deutsche Tourenwagen Meisterschaft, or German Touring Car Championship) gave further impetus to this, although the W201-based DTM car would not actually make its debut until 1986 (see Chapter 7).

Mercedes wasted no time in preparing the new high-performance W201 for production, although there were long delays before it was possible to buy one. The first 190s had been available for less than a year when a batch of five pilot-production models was built at Sindelfingen. Three of them were promptly used to take a series of speed records at the Nardo test track in Italy during August 1983.

By this stage, the internal name of 'Sport' had been dropped, and the car was announced at the Frankfurt show in September as the 190E 2.3-16. It was a name that made very clear what the engine was, but was too much of a mouthful for most people, so the car became far more widely known as the Cosworth Mercedes (especially in Britain), or as the '16-valve 190E'.

The Nardo record runs were a typical high-profile Mercedes publicity stunt, designed to attract worldwide attention (which they did, very successfully) and to emphasize the new model's performance and durability. The factory later claimed that the cars were standard, but they actually had a series of small modifications. To get the Cd down to 0.285 from the standard 0.32, the door mirrors had been removed, the ventilation had been blocked off, and the front end had been lowered by 45mm. The PAS pump had been deleted and the cars ran with an open exhaust, which allowed the engines to develop between 215 and 220PS. There were gearing changes, too, and all the cars had a tall 2.65:1 final drive to improve their maximum speed. Reverse had been deleted from the gearbox to save weight, and Pirelli had provided some special high-speed tyres.

Everything was meticulously organized, in the usual Mercedes fashion. The 150-strong team was led by development chief Guido Moch, with the legendary Mercedes competitions man Erich Waxenberger. A team of eighteen drivers ran the three cars flat out for eight days and nights, establishing twelve international endurance records. Nine were in Category D, for cars with engines smaller than 3 litres; the other three were distance records for 25,000km, 25,000 miles and 50,000km, over which the cars achieved a combined average speed of 154.06mph (247.94km/h). It was a hugely impressive début.

Even though the 16-valve engine was the key feature of the new 190E 2.3-16, Mercedes had certainly not missed any tricks in making the car look different from other W201s. Immediately obvious was a bodykit of aprons, spoilers and sills in the high-performance idiom of the day. These were not simply for visual effect: they had been developed in the wind tunnel and their combined effect was to reduce the car's Cd to 0.32 from the standard W201's 0.33. If that does not sound particularly impressive, they also reduced front-end lift by up to 47 per cent and rear-end lift by up to 40 per cent, to the benefit of handling at high speeds.

The aerodynamic addenda included a chin spoiler, side skirts below the sills, a spoiler on the boot lid and an apron below the rear bumper. The rear spoiler, which would soon be copied by aftermarket companies, was important for safety at high speed. Owners were strictly forbidden by Mercedes to take it off. Lower flank panels similar to those on the W126 S Class linked the front and rear aprons visually and ensured that the bodykit did not look like a cheap aftermarket add-on. All these elements were made of impact-absorbing laminated polyurethane, reinforced with alloy profiles in high-stress areas and impregnated with body colour. At this stage the colour-impregnating process had its limitations. As a result, Mercedes made the 16-valve car available in just two colours: metallic Smoke Silver (always unique to the Cosworth) and Blue-Black metallic (which was nearer to dark grey in most lights).

The passenger cabin made its own special contribution to the car's sporting demeanour. It came with four suitably supportive bucket-type seats that normally had check-pattern cloth inserts and vinyl bolsters, in a scheme that was echoed on the door trims. Leather or velour could be had at extra cost, and leather trim was standard on both the steering wheel and the gearshift grip. The steering wheel was 10mm smaller in diameter than on other 190s, complementing a quicker ratio and power-assisted rack, and there were three extra dials in a special centre console – an oil temperature gauge, a voltmeter and a digital clock with a stopwatch function. The speedometer read to 260km/h (or 160mph) and a rev counter with analogue clock was of course standard.

Taking endurance records with the car at the
Nardo track in Italy provided some valuable
early publicity for the new 190E 2.3-16 model.

Three cars were involved in the
endurance record runs; this is the second,
distinguished by red markings.

The third Nardo car, pictured many years later in November 2013 during a track
work-out. It was distinguished by markings that were originally white.

Mercedes had a reputation for slick and professional pit work; the team's
skills were in evidence again during the Nardo runs.

The Nardo cars carried some extra instrumentation,
which can be seen here in the centre below the
radio, which is, of course, a two-way type.

This early engine in one of the Nardo cars is
missing both the identification that characterized
the production versions, and the cover over
the ignition leads on top of the engine.

The 190E 2.3-16 certainly looked the part with its showroom specification.
The Blue-Black metallic really suited the car.

The alternative colour was Smoke Silver. The superb fit of the cladding panels on the lower
body is apparent even at this distance. The spoiler on the boot lid was discreet by later
standards, although it was quite a revelation at the time for Mercedes followers.

So what of that engine, which was guaranteed legendary status from the time Mercedes asked Cosworth to get involved with it? Its 2299cc swept volume was exactly the same as that of the parent M102 2.3-litre, and its cast-iron cylinder block was always made in Germany. It retained standard con-rods, bearings and bearing caps, but came with special Mahle forged light-alloy pistons and reinforced rings that allowed it to operate safely at its 7,000rpm redline. Always assembled in Stuttgart, its cylinder heads were cast and partly assembled in Britain, then finally machined at their destination.

The two rows of valves in the cylinder head were set at 45 degrees to one another, the inlet valves having a 38mm diameter while the sodium-cooled exhaust valves had a 33mm diameter. The inlet valves opened for 37 per cent longer than on the standard engine and the exhaust valves opened for 43 per cent longer. Neither had hydraulic tappets, so

the valve clearances needed attention at routine services, and everything was arranged so that the camshafts could be removed easily. Both inlet and exhaust manifolds were complex pieces of plumbing and RHD versions of the car had a special tubular exhaust manifold (known at Stuttgart as the English Hunting Horn) to clear the steering column. The original design for this caused some power loss and as a result production of RHD cars was delayed while it was redesigned. British buyers had to wait until autumn 1985 to get their hands on a Cosworth Mercedes. When they did, the selection of auxiliary instruments was different from that on the German cars, with an outside temperature gauge in place of the digital clock with its stopwatch function.

The engine in the road cars produced 185PS – a quite spectacular figure for the period – yet it was in fact quite heavily detuned from the competition unit that Cosworth had developed as their WAA type. This was supposedly drawn

The 16-valve car was stunningly attractive from all angles. The overhead view shows that the body addenda did not detract in any way from the sleekness or neatness of the original car.

49

An engine with the identification, and the ignition lead cover in place.

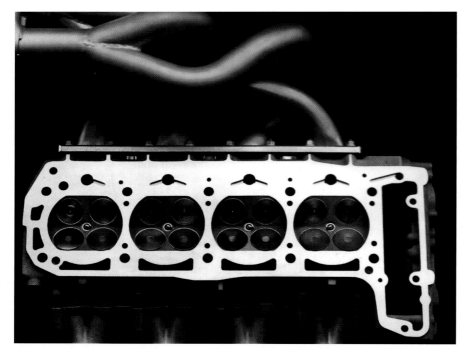

Four valves per cylinder have since become commonplace, but in the early 1980s the set-up represented modern technology for a road car.

up with a target figure of 325PS and had certainly developed 280PS on the test bench. It had been designed around the largest valves that could physically be fitted into the combustion chamber, with a dry sump lubrication system and a Kugelfischer injection system. For the road cars, it had smaller-diameter inlet and exhaust ports, different camshaft profiles, a conventional wet sump, and a Bosch KE-Jetronic injection system.

The 16-valve engine put its power down through a 35 per cent limited-slip differential and a Getrag five-speed close-ratio gearbox with direct top gear that had a dog's-leg gate (left and back for first gear) and a rather slow and imprecise change. Unsurprisingly, an oil cooler was standard equipment. A 70-litre fuel tank replaced the standard 55-litre type to maintain a good cruising range: Mercedes had no illusions about the way these cars were going to be driven even if the four-valve layout did offer some fuel-saving advantages.

Both front and rear anti-roll bars were fatter than standard, and the brakes came with ventilated discs at the front and solid discs at the rear; although ABS was not standard on the first cars, it became so in December 1984. Suspension mounting points were reinforced and the ride height was lowered by 15mm, while there was a slight increase in the negative camber of the rear wheels and self-levelling rear suspension was standard. With fat 205/55 VR 15 Pirelli P6 tyres on 16-hole alloy wheels, power-assisted steering was essential, and the wider tracks also demanded slightly flared wheel arches. The steering was actually more direct than on a standard 190E, with a 15.27:1 ratio instead of the standard 16.66:1; for those who insisted, a 3.27:1 final drive could be ordered.

It all made for an astonishingly tempting package, but it would be another year

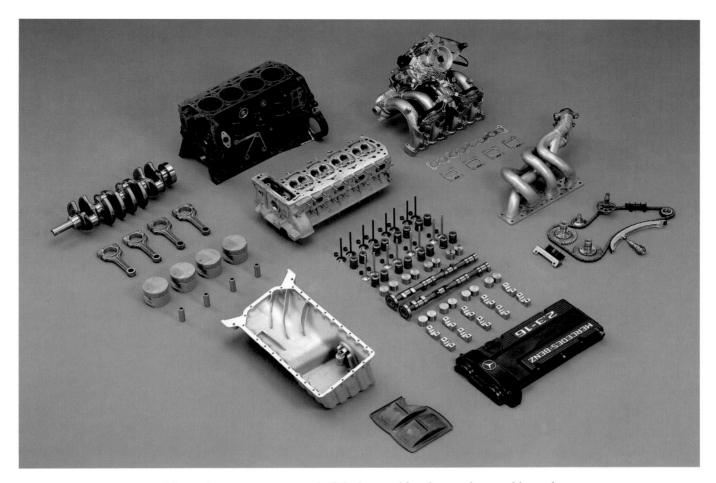

**Mercedes were very proud of their new 16-valve engine, and issued
several publicity pictures showing its components.**

before it actually went on sale, with Mercedes muttering darkly about delays caused by Cosworth's failures to meet their quality demands with the special cylinder heads. Volume production of the 2.3-16 did not begin at Sindelfingen until September 1984. The original plan was to build just the 5,000 cars needed to homologate the Cosworth for Group A touring car events, but its makers had rather underestimated the interest that the car would generate. So popular did the 190E 2.3-16 become that early cars were still selling for more than their cost price a year after showroom sales had begun!

As a result, Mercedes changed its plans. Instead of ending production after the required 5,000 cars had been assembled at Sindelfingen, they looked at switching production to the Bremen plant. The 5,000th car was built in May 1985 and

in that same month the first 16-valve Mercedes came off the new lines in Bremen. Production continued at Sindelfingen for a further three months before the lines were closed down and the job was left entirely to Bremen. By the end of 1985, the two factories had built no fewer than 11,000 examples between them.

Conscious that the effect of the September 1983 launch would eventually wear off, Mercedes wanted to make sure that the public was reminded about the 16-valve car before showroom sales began. In the early summer of 1984, the company teamed up with the owners of the Nürburgring race track, which was being re-opened in May with a new Grand Prix circuit. On 12 May 1984, Mercedes held a 'celebration' invitation-only one-make Race of Champions that featured twenty identical pilot-production 2.3-16s. The cars

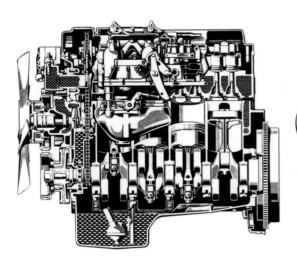

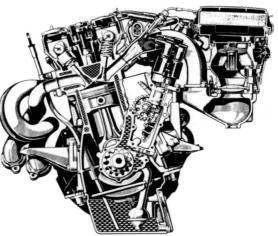

Cutaway drawings like these were standard Mercedes publicity fare. The standard exhaust manifold was convoluted enough: on the right-hand-drive cars it was even worse, and stood a little higher to clear the steering column.

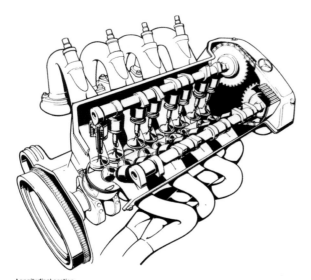

Longitudinal-section

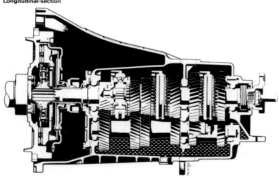

Cutaways showing the twin-cam arrangement of the 16-valve engine and the layout of the close-ratio five-speed gearbox that accompanied it.

were almost to showroom specification, with only a set of racing bucket seats and harnesses, a simple roll-cage, a 15mm lower ride height and a shorter final drive. A glittering array of current and future racing stars to drive them would guarantee maximum publicity, which was exactly what Mercedes wanted.

The drivers included Niki Lauda, Stirling Moss, Jacques Laffite, Alain Prost, Carlos Reutemann, Elio de Angelis, Keke Rosberg, John Surtees and James Hunt. Alongside them was the eventual race winner, a young Brazilian named Ayrton Senna. It is often said that this race was the first one in which Senna displayed his prodigious talents, but in fact he was already becoming known to motorsport enthusiasts, having won the British Formula 3 Championship and raced in four Grands Prix. Many of the Nürburgring vehicles were displayed at dealerships for a time, while Senna's winning car was handed over to the Mercedes-Benz Museum.

Press Reaction to the 190E Cosworth

Just how fast was the original Cosworth Mercedes? There was no doubt that in 1984 it was one of the fastest saloon cars in the world. The factory claims were a top speed of 230km/h (143mph) and a 0–100km/h standing start time of 7.5 seconds. Individual cars varied a little, as always, and when the Belgian magazine *Le Moniteur de L'Automobile* tried one, it recorded 233km/h (144.7mph) and 0–100km/h in 7.9 seconds. In Britain, *Motor* magazine of 10 August 1985 reported a slightly disappointing mean maximum speed of 137.1mph, with a 0–60mph time of 7.4 seconds.

Autocar did better when it tested one for its issue dated 7 August 1985. It achieved a best figure of 145mph with a mean maximum speed of exactly the 143mph that Mercedes quoted. The 0–60mph time was exactly eight seconds.

This British magazine felt that the Cosworth was 'exactly how you would expect Mercedes-Benz to build a sports car...thoroughly competent, well-engineered [and] dynami-

cally excellent'. Although it was 'hardly exciting in the way it performs', it was 'a taut sports saloon, every inch an enthusiast's car, entirely forgiving in its *in extremis* handling, thoroughly enjoyable to drive hard'. The testers reflected that 'perhaps Mercedes has retained too much of the refinement of the normal 190 series, so the 2.3-16 just doesn't feel or sound as quick as it is'.

The car could be 'driven in a quiet, refined, round-town manner, and any light-footed owner should expect to get

The Race of Champions at the re-opening of the Nürburgring in May 1984 featured a fleet of mechanically identical 16-valve models. It was won by the then relatively unknown Brazilian driver Ayrton Senna.

Senna's winning car from 1984 has been carefully preserved by Mercedes-Benz Classic.

Carlos Reuteman was among the participants in the 1984 Nürburgring race. This picture shows what appears to have been a decal trial; the car carries the registration plate that has been used on Stuttgart's styling models for very many years.

better than 25mpg in normal use': a 'very flat torque curve means that the engine runs efficiently through much of its rev range, and also leads to the sort of flexibility that allows the car to pull away from as low as 10mph in fourth with very little hesitation or vibration'. It sounded refined, too, with some 'induction roar during acceleration, but blended with a burr from the exhaust which is neither rorty nor raspy'.

Meanwhile, 'behind the wheel all is normal, quality, refined and subdued Mercedes'. Handling was characterized by mild understeer, although in hard cornering 'the tail will drift out, ever so gently, to allow exhilarating throttle-controlled oversteer cornering. The beauty of the 190 is that the transition back from oversteer to understeer is also so incredibly gentle.'

Inevitably, there were some negative comments. First, the high price came in for criticism: at £21,000, the Cosworth was nearly as expensive as an Audi Quattro coupé, and that was before extras were added to the Mercedes. *Autocar* also felt that the steering was rather dead around the straight-

ahead position, and complained that kick-back set up a gentle oscillation of the steering wheel in fast corners. Last, the gearbox was described as both notchy and baulky. According to the reviewer, 'The change quality of the Getrag unit is nothing like as slick as such an arrangement [a dog's-leg] ideally should be.'

THE 1985 MODELS

The Frankfurt motor show in September 1984 was held just nine months after the launch of the W201s, in December 1983, and the 190 variants shown there as 1985 models incorporated a number of revisions that had been made as the result of customer feedback. A month or so later, Mercedes would announce the new medium-sized saloons of the W124 that would replace the long-serving W123 range. This had been developed to use much of the technology originally designed for the W201 models, and it shared the new, clean and aerodynamic look that Bruno Sacco had created for the compact models.

Outside North America, the W201 range increased to four when the 190E 2.3-16 became available. Those four models were the 190, 190E, 190D and the new 16-valve car. Later in the 1985 season would come a fifth model, another diesel, named the 190D 2.5. There were also special models for North America (*see* Chapter 6); right-hand-drive variants of the 2.3-16 became available for Britain and other markets in July 1985.

Both the 190 and 190E versions of the M102 engine were modified for 1985 with hydraulic valve adjusters, which took up clearances as components wore and so removed one task from the servicing schedule. All the engines now took on the single auxiliary belt that had been pioneered on the 190D, replacing the earlier multiple-belt drives: cars with PAS had needed two separate belts, and models with air conditioning had needed three. The single belt was now expected to last for 100,000km (62,000 miles), which again reduced the need for maintenance attention. Cars with PAS now simply had a longer belt than non-PAS models, to cope with the additional pulley. There was also a change to the oil filter,

as a disposable-element type replaced the cartridge type on early engines.

The 1985-season carburettor 190s also had a very welcome power increase. Perhaps the plan had always been to replace the original 90PS engine after the first nine months, once the distinction had become established between the 190 and the 200 model of the medium-sized range. One way or another, what was known internally as a '190/1' had 105PS for 1985. Its engine was in fact the same as that in the new W124 200, although that had 4PS more, thanks to a less restrictive exhaust system. The peak torque figure remained unchanged. These engine revisions were also carried over for the special export variant designed to cope with low-octane and lead-free petrol, which now boasted 99PS – more than the original 'standard' 190.

According to the German magazine *Auto, Motor und Sport*, the 1985-model 190 had a top speed of 193km/h (120mph), as against the 185km/h (115mph) that its manufacturer claimed. The manual-gearbox car took 11.6 seconds to reach 100km/h from rest and the automatic model took a second longer. Meanwhile, autumn 1984 also saw the release of a little-known (and probably little-loved) version

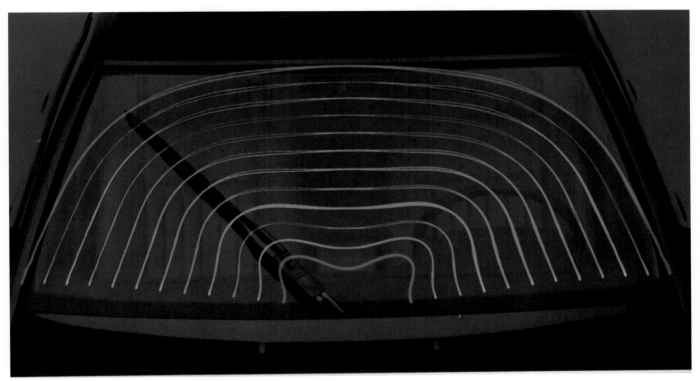

Mercedes were masters at creating graphics to illustrate engineering features. This one showed how the new 'jumping' (or crank-action) windscreen wiper worked.

of the 190E with a catalytic converter. There was already, of course, a 'cat'-equipped W201 for North America, but that had the larger and more powerful 2.3-litre engine. This model seems to have been intended to gauge the likely effect on W201 buyers of forthcoming West German legislation to make catalytic converters compulsory. With a compression ratio lowered to just 8.0:1 and performance commensurate with that, it did not sell well and was available for only about ten months before being withdrawn. However, a full-production 190E with catalytic converter was already on the way.

Not all the 1985 revisions to the W201 affected the engines. There were also some interior changes. Seat-belt tensioners, which had been an option on the earlier cars, now became standard on all models. There were new dashboard warning lights for oil, coolant and washer fluid levels, and another addition to the options list was electric adjustment for the front seats, with a memory as well.

Even then, Mercedes did not manage to get all the 1985-season revisions ready in time for the Frankfurt Show in autumn 1984. Three changes were held over until January 1985. One of these was the standardization of electrically heated washer jets, which was certainly welcome but was nowhere near as far-reaching as the other two. These had both been introduced on the new W124 models a few months earlier. One affected the windscreen wiper. Although the single wiper on the first cars represented some advanced thinking, it was also not quite as efficient as it might have been. It actually swept only 75 per cent of the screen, 3 per cent less than the twin wipers of the W123-series cars. A similar single-wiper system was employed for the W124 models, but it had been modified to cover an impressive 86 per cent of the screen – an area greater than that on any other production car of the time. This modified system was also adopted for the W201 from January 1985. It retained a single blade, but now incorporated an eccentric to lift that blade as it approached the top corners of the windscreen, returning to its normal reach afterwards to avoid a foul with the windscreen pillars. At the same time, a heated washer jet with three nozzles became standard equipment.

The second change in January 1985 was to 15-inch wheels – the same size as on the W124s – from the 14-inch wheels of the early cars. These were accompanied by low-profile tyres. The steel wheels retained flush-fitting polyamide trims and the optional alloys still had a sixteen-hole design, so that the change made no real difference to the appearance of the cars. For Mercedes and its suppliers, however, it

brought a welcome streamlining of logistics and parts stockage, because both W124 and W201 models now shared wheels and, to a lesser extent, tyres.

A third and much less visible change in early 1985 was the addition of a heat shield to the exhaust in order to protect the paint at the rear of the car. On early cars, this had proved to be prone to deterioration.

A FIFTH MODEL: THE 190D 2.5

A New Addition to the Range

Among the engine options for the new W124 saloons that were announced in November 1984 was a five-cylinder diesel with a 2.5-litre capacity, which powered a model called the 250D. There was no indication at the start of the season that this was also destined for the W201 range, but it was introduced before the season was over, to create a fifth model in the range.

In fact, pilot production of the model that would become the 190D 2.5 had already delivered forty-six cars during August. Full production would begin at Sindelfingen in April 1985 and at Bremen in May, which was the month in which the new model was announced. Mercedes needed this addition to the W201 range for several reasons. One was to counter the new diesel-engined BMW 3 Series, which had been launched at the 1983 Frankfurt show in 2.4-litre turbocharged form as the 324td. The other was to streamline production by replacing the 190D 2.2, the special version of the 190D that was available only in North America.

Mercedes was familiar with five-cylinder diesel engines, having had one in its medium-sized saloons since 1974. All production of the new five-cylinder diesel unit was initially earmarked for the W124 range, which was no surprise, but as soon as production volumes had built up, the engine appeared in the W201s. It was of course a five-cylinder version of the modular diesel engine range that had been introduced with the OM601 four-cylinder, which was giving sterling service in the 190D. It became known as the OM602. Later, there would be a 3.0-litre six-cylinder OM603 as well, although not for the W201.

The new OM602 diesel engine weighed just 18kg (39.6lb) more than its four-cylinder sibling, but it was enough for Mercedes to consider that power-assisted steering needed to be standard. With 18PS more than the 2.0-litre diesel, and with high torque of 154Nm low down at 2,000rpm, it delivered performance that would have been unthinkable for a diesel car at the turn of the 1980s. It was also a much smoother engine than the OM601 four-cylinder. The 190D 2.5 was offered with the five-speed overdrive manual gearbox, to give good economy, or at extra cost with the four-speed automatic, for greater ease of driving.

BMW countered at Frankfurt in the autumn with a naturally aspirated version of their six-cylinder diesel, in a model called the 324d. However, with just 86PS against the 90PS of the Mercedes engine, it was less powerful; it also proved to be thirstier, although its quite remarkable smoothness and refinement did win it many friends. None of that prevented the success of the 190D 2.5, and by the end of 1985 the model was accounting for 12.5 per cent of all diesel W201s sold globally. It was a good total, in view of the fact that the model was significantly more costly than the 190D.

Press Reaction to the 190D 2.5

As so often happened, Mercedes' official performance figures were bettered by the press when they subjected examples of the 190D 2.5 to full tests. The factory figures for both the five-speed and automatic cars were a maximum speed of 174km/h (108mph) and a 0–100km/h time of 15.1 seconds. Austrian *Autorevue* magazine was among those that proved these figures to be conservative, with their test achieving a maximum of 177km/h (110mph) and 14.3 seconds for the 0–100km/h sprint.

Right-hand-drive cars for Britain were not available until January 1986, and it was 23 August before *Motor* magazine tested one with the five-speed manual gearbox. At the time, diesel-engined cars accounted for no more than 4 per cent of the entire British market, so the 190D 2.5 was never going to be a strong seller. Its value to the average motorist

The five-cylinder diesel engine introduced for the 190D 2.5 was from the same modular family as the four-cylinder 2.0-litre in the 190D. All five characteristic curved inlet tracts can be seen here. DEZ1172/WIKIMEDIA COMMONS

was also questionable, according to *Motor*: 'Based on our overall fuel consumption figures, the 190D 2.5 would take around 130,000 miles to reach a break-even point compared with the petrol-engined 190 on fuel costs alone. But there will also be small savings on maintenance costs and lower […] insurances.'

Nevertheless, it was deemed to be 'a much better proposition than the four-cylinder 190 diesel'. Even though it 'must still be judged slow by absolute standards […], gear for gear, the 2.5 diesel keeps pace with the petrol-engined 190, though it relies on shorter gearing to achieve it.' The car 'can at least keep up with the general flow of traffic, and there's enough power in reserve to maintain cruising speed up motorway inclines.' It was not particularly noisy: 'Subjectively, the engine gets loud when accelerating hard, though it's better than the two-litre diesel whose engine had to be permanently hard worked. The noise abates to a barely audible thrum when cruising.' With a best maximum speed of 106.1mph and a 0–60mph time of 15.1 seconds, the 190D 2.5 returned a 'creditable' 35.6mpg.

TECHNICAL SPECIFICATIONS: MERCEDES-BENZ W201 MODELS, 1982–1985

Engine (190)
M102 four-cylinder with cast-iron block and alloy cylinder head
1997cc (89mm bore × 80.25mm stroke)
Single overhead camshaft, two valves per cylinder
Five-bearing crankshaft
Compression ratio 9.0:1 (9.1:1 from October 1984)
Stromberg 175 CDT carburettor
Max. power 90PS at 5,200rpm (105PS/5,200 from October 1984)
Max. torque 170Nm at 2,500rpm

Engine (190E)
M102E four-cylinder with cast-iron block and alloy cylinder head
1997cc (89mm bore × 80.25mm stroke)
Single overhead camshaft, two valves per cylinder
Five-bearing crankshaft
Compression ratio 9.1:1
Bosch K-Jetronic mechanical fuel injection
Max. power 122PS at 5,100rpm
Max. torque 174Nm at 3,500rpm

Engine (190D)
OM601 four-cylinder diesel with cast-iron block and alloy cylinder head
1997cc (87mm bore × 84mm stroke)
Single overhead camshaft, two valves per cylinder

Five-bearing crankshaft
Compression ratio 22:1
Indirect injection with Bosch pump
Max. power 72PS at 4,600rpm
Max. torque 123Nm at 2,800rpm

Engine (190E 2.3-16)
M102 four-cylinder with cast-iron block and alloy cylinder head
2299cc (95mm bore × 80.25mm stroke)
Two overhead camshafts, four valves per cylinder
Five-bearing crankshaft
Compression ratio 10.2:1
Bosch KE-Jetronic mechanical fuel injection
Max. power 185PS at 6,000rpm
Max. torque 235Nm at 4,500rpm

Engine (190D 2.5)
OM602 five-cylinder with cast-iron block and alloy cylinder head
2497cc (87mm bore × 84mm stroke)
Single overhead camshaft, two valves per cylinder
Six-bearing crankshaft
Compression ratio 22:1
Indirect injection with Bosch pump
Max. power 90PS at 4,600rpm
Max. torque 154Nm at 2,800rpm

Gearbox
Four-speed manual GL68/20 C (190E to August 1983)
    Ratios 3.91:1, 2.32:1, 1.42:1, 1.00:1, reverse 3.78:1
Four-speed manual GL68/20 G (190, 190E from August 1983)

INTERIOR COLOURS FOR W201 MODELS, 1982–1985

Upholstery was available in Cloth, MB-Tex, Velours or (from January 1984) Leather. The seven-colour range was initially Black, Blue, Brazil, Date, Cream, Dark Olive and Henna Red. Cream and Henna Red were withdrawn in December 1984; from January 1985, they were replaced by Cream Beige and Mid Red. Grey was added at the same time to make the total colour options up to eight. Notably, Velours never came in Black, but in Anthracite.

Ratios 3.91:1, 2.17:1, 1.37:1, 1.00:1, reverse 3.78:1
Four-speed manual GL68/20 D (190D)
Ratios 4.23:1, 2.36:1, 1.49:1, 1.00:1, reverse 4.10:1
Five-speed manual GL68/20 B-5 (190, 190E, 190D 2.5)
Ratios 3.91:1, 2.17:1, 1.37:1, 1.00:1, 0.78:1, reverse 4.27:1
Five-speed manual GL68/20 A-5 (190D)
Ratios 4.23:1, 2.36:1, 1.49:1, 1.00:1, 0.84:1, reverse 4.63:1
Five-speed close-ratio manual (190E 2.3-16)
Ratios 4.08:1, 2.52:1, 1.77:1, 1.26:1, 1.00:1, reverse 4.16:1
Four-speed automatic W4A 020 (190, 190E, 190D, 190D 2.5)
Ratios 4.25:1, 2.41:1, 1.49:1, 1.00:1, reverse 5.67:1

Axle ratio
3.23:1 (190, 190E, 190D)
3.64:1 (190D 2.5 five-speed)
3.07:1 (190E 2.3-16, 190D 2.5 automatic)

Suspension
Front suspension with MacPherson struts, wishbones, coil springs, telescopic gas dampers and anti-roll bar.
Rear suspension with five links, coil springs, telescopic gas dampers and anti-roll bar; hydro-pneumatic self-levelling strut standard on 190E 2.3-16 and optional on other models.

Steering
Recirculating-ball steering with optional power assistance (standard on 190E 2.3-16 and 190D 2.5).

Brakes
Disc brakes on all four wheels, ventilated at the front on 190E 2.3-16; dual hydraulic circuit and servo assistance; ABS optional (standard on 190E 2.3-16 from December 1984).

Dimensions
Overall length: 4,420mm (4,430mm for 190E 2.3-16)
Overall width: 1,678 mm (1,706mm for 190E 2.3-16)
Overall height: 1,383mm to December 1984
1,390mm from January 1985
1,361mm for 190E 2.3-16
Wheelbase: 2,665mm
Track, front: 1,428mm to December 1984
1,437mm from January 1985
1,445mm for 190E 2.3-16
Track, rear: 1,415mm to December 1984
1,418mm from January 1985
1,429mm for 190E 2.3-16

Wheels and tyres
5J × 14 steel disc wheels with 175/70 R 14 tyres, to December 1984
5J × 14 alloy wheels with 175/70 R 14 tyres optional, to December 1984
6J × 15 steel disc wheels with 185/65 R 15 tyres, from January 1985
6J × 15 alloy wheels with 185/65 R 15 tyres optional on 190, 190E and 190D, from January 1985
7J × 15 alloy wheels with 205/55 VR 15 tyres, for 190E 2.3-16

Running weight
190: 1,080kg (to December 1984); 1,110kg (from January 1985)
190E: 1,100kg (to December 1984); 1,130kg (from January 1985)
190D: 1,110kg (to December 1984); 1,130kg (from January 1985)
190E 2.3-16: 1,260kg
190D 2.5: 1,175kg

Paint Colours for W201 Models, 1983–1985

German name	English name	Code	Model-year		
			1983	1984	1985
Beige					
Hellelfenbein	Taxi Beige/Light Ivory	623	✓	✓	✓
Taigabeige	Taiga Beige	684	✓	✓	✓
Black					
Schwarz	Black	040	✓	✓	✓
Blue					
Diamantblau	Diamond Blue	355		✓	✓
Dunkelblau	Midnight Blue	904	✓	✓	✓
Labradorblau	Labrador Blue	312	✓	✓	
Nautikblau	Nautical Blue metallic	929		✓	✓
Petrol	Blue-green metallic	877	✓	✓	✓
Silberblau	Blue Silver	930	✓		
Surfblau	Surf Blue	900	✓	✓	✓
Brown					
Braun	Russet Brown	427	✓		
Champagner	Champagne metallic	473	✓	✓	✓
Manganbraun	Manganese Brown	480	✓	✓	✓
Maroonbraun	Maroon Brown	459		✓	✓
Green					
Eibengrün	Forest Green	822	✓	✓	✓
Riedgrün	Moss Green	803	✓	✓	✓
Silberdistel	Thistle Green metallic	881	✓	✓	✓
Zypressengrün	Cypress Green metallic	876	✓	✓	✓
Grey					
Anthrazitgrau	Anthracite Grey	172	✓	✓	✓
Blauschwarz	Blue-Black metallic	199		✓	✓
Liasgrau	Grey	751	✓	✓	✓
Red					
Altrot	Mesa Red	585	✓		
Barolorot	Barolo Red	540		✓	✓
Orientrot	Orient Red	501	✓	✓	
Pajettrot	Pajett Red metallic	587		✓	✓
Signalrot	Signal Red	568	✓	✓	✓
Silver					
Astralsilber	Astral Silver	735	✓	✓	✓
Rauchsilber	Smoke Silver	702		✓	✓
White					
Arcticweiss	Arctic White				✓
Classicweiss	Classic White	737	✓	✓	
Yellow					
Hellocker	Light Ochre	690			✓
Saharagelb	Sahara Yellow	673	✓		
Weizengelb	Manila Beige	681	✓	✓	

Note: Rauchsilber was available only on the 190E 2.3-16.

CHAPTER THREE

SECOND STAGE:
THE 1986–1988 MODEL 201s

Mercedes entered the 1986 model-year with five variants of the W201 in production for Europe. Three – the 190, the 190E and the 190E 2.3-16 – had petrol engines; the other two were the diesel-powered 190D and 190D 2.5. For North America, there was a petrol-engined 190E 2.3, and there was also a new emissions-controlled variant of the Cosworth model. It was certainly complicated on the assembly lines in Stuttgart and Bremen, and it was about to get worse, as new variants were introduced to meet forthcoming emissions-control regulations in West Germany.

NEW VARIANTS FOR NEW REGULATIONS

German political pursuit of environmental and clean-air policies was already well established by the early 1980s, when the first members of the Green Party were elected to the Federal Parliament. Their influence spread, and within a few years the country had legislation in place that required all new petrol-engined cars to have catalytic converters in their exhaust systems from 1989. The new requirements would be phased in gradually and, from 1 January 1986, unleaded petrol would be introduced to West Germany and car buyers would be offered financial incentives to buy catalyst-equipped cars.

The catalytic converter in place. It reduced the power output of the 16-valve engine by around 3PS, to some extent because of a lower compression ratio.

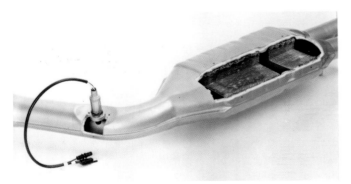

The catalytic converter for a 16-valve car, cut away to show its internals. It was made available by Mercedes for 1986, to comply with new regulations that would require all petrol-engined cars sold in West Germany from 1989 to have a 'cat' in the exhaust. The wire seen here is for the Lambda probe, or oxygen sensor.

The principle was the same for all W201 models. This was the catalytic converter of a standard 2.0-litre two-valve 190E

Mercedes responded to these requirements in their own way, with a view to minimizing complication on the assembly lines. In autumn 1985, domestic-market variants of most models were introduced with a catalytic converter. These were known as KAT types. In addition, there were variants that came with an engine management system that meant they were capable of running with a catalytic converter and Lambda probe, although they did not actually have these items fitted; the idea was that they could be made to meet requirements at a later date by having the converter and probe fitted by a Mercedes dealer. These were known as RÜF types, an abbreviation of *Rückrüstfahrzeug*, or 'retrospective fit car'. For markets outside West Germany where there was no requirement for catalytic converters, models continued to be built in the old way; these were known as ECE (European Community) types.

Cars with the RÜF specification ran on traditional leaded fuel, but were also fitted with an octane selector under the bonnet that allowed them to run safely on low-octane unleaded petrol. When a catalytic converter was fitted, this was set permanently to suit low-octane petrol. The differences in power output between the RÜF and KAT models were minimal, which indicated how much engine technology had advanced since the early days of catalytic converters for the USA, which had reduced power outputs to an enormous extent.

The plan had been to announce RÜF and KAT variants of all three petrol-engined W201s at the Frankfurt show in September 1985, but in practice the new variant of the entry-level 190 was held over. A disastrous fire at the Neuss factory of Pierburg, which had been contracted to supply its new carburettor, delayed the start of production until April 1986. However, the 190E KAT did make an appearance, and replaced the earlier 190E KAT that had been available during the 1985 model-year. With 118PS, this more considered model was only 4PS down on the ECE and RÜF models. When the Swiss *Automobil Revue* tested an automatic 190E KAT in 1985, they recorded a top speed of 193km/h, which was just 2km/h less than Mercedes claimed for the ECE and RÜF models. The 0–100km/h time of 11.3 seconds was barely different from the factory's claim of 11.0 seconds for the cars without a catalytic converter.

There were RÜF and KAT variants of the 16-valve car as well, in each case with new pistons that gave a lower compression ratio of 9.7:1 (while the ECE cars retained the original pistons and 10.5:1 compression ratio). While the ECE model that remained in production for export continued

to boast 185PS at 6,200rpm, the RÜF model had 177PS at 5,800rpm and the full KAT version had 170PS at 5,800rpm, which was exactly the same as the version that was released for North America at the same time.

It was no surprise, then, that Mercedes took the precaution of lowering the final drive ratio on all except the ECE models to 3.27:1, which offset the loss of acceleration to some extent. Top speeds were down, of course: an ECE car was still capable of 230km/h (143mph), but the RÜF model peaked at 225km/h (140mph) and the KAT variant was down to 220km/h (137mph). When the Swiss *Automobil Revue* tried a 190E 2.3-16 KAT model with the standard manual gearbox, they managed a top speed of 221km/h (137mph) and took 7.8 seconds to reach 100km/h from rest.

The Cosworth car's woes were not yet over. BMW also chose the 1985 Frankfurt show to announce their new M3 model as a direct rival for the 190E 2.3-16. Although this variant of the strong-selling 3 Series would not reach the showrooms for another year, nobody doubted that its purpose was to steal Mercedes' thunder – and in due course it would go on to do exactly that. The two car makers were constantly jockeying for position at this time and Mercedes had made sure that they, too, had not one but two exciting new compact saloon variants to announce at Frankfurt in 1985. In common with the BMW M3, neither was yet on sale, but the six-cylinder 190E 2.6 would enter production just seven months later, in April 1986. The 190E 2.3, meanwhile, was a European version of the car that had been sold in the USA since 1984, and would actually reach the showrooms a year later, as a 1987 model.

The headlines at Frankfurt were clear, but Mercedes also announced some incremental improvements to the W201 range. Most important was the move to make power-assisted steering standard on all models. At the same time, electrically heated door mirrors (which came on with the heated rear window) were also made standard across the range. There were some ratio changes in the 190D's optional five-speed manual gearbox, which improved the car's acceleration through the gears, and an adjustable front suspension was introduced as an option for the Cosworth model. Intended mainly for cars used in competition, this gave three different ride heights at the front, lowering the nose a little to improve airflow.

There would be more changes to the range in the new year, but in the mean time sales of the W201 models surged ahead. During the 1985 calendar-year, sales in Germany exceeded those of the rival BMW 3 Series by 26 per cent.

Unsurprisingly, the strongest demand world-wide was for the 190E. On 15 November 1985, the half-millionth W201 left the assembly lines in Sindelfingen. It was an impressive total in just under three years of production, but some way below the 764,124 3 Series BMWs built in the same period. Exports were still strong and Britain had established itself firmly as the best market for the W201 range outside Germany.

The changes in the first half of the 1986 calendar-year began in January, with the standardization of hardened valve seats in all petrol engines to allow the use of lead-free petrol. From March, the Cosworth model was offered with the option of an automatic gearbox. This was something that Mercedes had resisted for as long as they could, but there was no denying the existence of a group of customers who wanted the top specification in everything, and that meant combining the high performance of the 16-valve engine with the convenience of an automatic gearbox.

The gearbox chosen was of course a variant of the W4A 20 used in other W201s. It was accompanied by a propshaft that was 10mm fatter than the one in the manual-gearbox cars. The final drive was unchanged from the manual model, with a 3.07 ratio for the ECE model but a 3.27 for the RÜF and KAT variants. Maximum speeds were claimed to be 5km/h (about 3mph) down on equivalent manual models; an ECE Cosworth automatic despatched the 0–100km/h sprint in 7.8 seconds, but the RÜF car needed 8.2 seconds and the KAT model took 8.5 seconds.

THE 190E 2.6

A Six-Cylinder Version

The introduction of the W201 compact range for 1983 had seriously intensified the rivalry between Mercedes-Benz and BMW, and over the next few years the two companies missed no opportunities to score points off one another. When examples of the 190E 2.3-16 began to enter touring car racing in Europe (see Chapter 7), BMW hit back with the M3. So when BMW announced their 171PS six-cylinder 325i as the new top model of the 3 Series range in July 1985, Mercedes decided to strike back. Whether their new car had actually been in preparation before the 325i became public knowledge is not clear, but it was undoubtedly intended to steal some of the attention away from BMW's new M3 at Frankfurt in September 1985.

The 100,000th W201 was built at Sindelfingen in November 1985, just after the start of the 1986 model-year. It is pictured here against a background of other 190s and of their larger brethren, the medium-sized W124 saloons.

Mercedes' new offer was a six-cylinder W201, clearly a model that had been put together not long before the show. The W201 had not been designed to take a six-cylinder engine, but the 190D 2.5, introduced only a few months earlier in 1985, had proved that there was enough room in the engine bay for a five-cylinder. In practice, the Mercedes engineers were able to persuade the even longer six-cylinder to fit with just a minimum of adaptations. They modified the front panel and moved the radiator forward, mounting it on new supports that were bolted to the bodyshell rather than welded as on the four-cylinder cars. With a little careful relocation of ancillaries, the six-cylinder was successfully squeezed in, most importantly without adversely affecting the 201's crash performance.

The six-cylinder engine was about 20kg (44lb) heavier than the four-cylinder M102 types, so some suspension changes had to be made in order to restore the handling balance. Stuttgart's engineers fitted stronger springs and stiffer dampers, together with thicker anti-roll bars at front and rear. They fitted ventilated front disc brakes (although not the larger ones used on the Cosworth), and specified VR-rated tyres to suit the car's higher speed capability. The 190E 2.6 did not have ABS when announced at Frankfurt in autumn 1985, but by the time it actually entered production the anti-lock system had been made standard.

Size apparently did not matter... the 190s soon became a common sight at taxi ranks around the world, just as their larger forebears had done. This one is pictured at Peja in north-western Kosovo. DIMSFIKAS/WIKI/MEDIA CC 3.0

The cars were even adopted by police forces. This one, looking rather the worse for wear and apparently with bumper aprons from a later model, belonged to the police in Macedonia. DICKELBERS/WIKIMEDIA COMMONS

With relatively little persuasion, the 2.6-litre six-cylinder M103 engine was squeezed into the engine bay of the 190 to create a new top model for the mainstream 190 range.

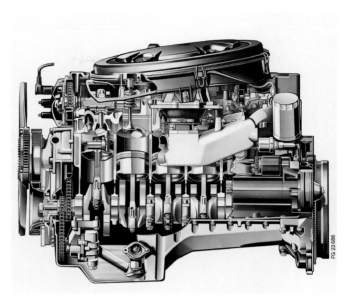

Another one of Mercedes' favoured cutaway drawings illustrates the internal layout of the M103 engine, which was related to the four-cylinder M102.

As for the engine itself, it was of course already in production by autumn 1985. It was an M103 type with 2599cc, initially developed for the 260E variant of the medium-sized W124 range and also available in the entry-level W126 S Class, the 260SE. Like the four-cylinder M102 types in the W201 range, the M103 engines had cast-iron cylinder blocks with aluminium alloy cylinder heads, and single overhead camshafts. Although Mercedes six-cylinder engines traditionally had a crankshaft that ran in seven bearings, the M103 had been designed with just four. This piece of design had been influenced by the principles of the Mercedes Energy Concept, which had been announced in 1981. Its advantage was that the smaller number of bearings reduced internal friction and therefore (by a tiny amount) increased the efficiency of the engine. Careful design elsewhere had meanwhile ensured that there was no loss of the smoothness expected of a six-cylinder engine. The M103 was undoubtedly one of the best passenger-car engines that Mercedes had produced up to that time.

There were two variants of it, the other being a 3.0-litre size in the 300E and related models. This larger engine had siamesed bores but the smaller-bore 2.6 had water between all the bores. The two engines shared their 80.25mm stroke with the four-cylinder M102 types. They had two valves per cylinder, a chain-driven camshaft, and a long poly-vee belt for the ancillaries, the latter like the latest versions of the four-cylinder. Their cross-flow cylinder heads were made of aluminium alloy and the Bosch KE-Jetronic injection system (also known by the name of CIS-E) was essentially the same as that used on the 190E.

The external differences between the six-cylinder car and the four- and five-cylinder models were subtle; only the front apron identifies this one as a six-cylinder from this angle.

When the front apron was hard to see, as here, the six-cylinder car looked the same as the other models. Note the four head restraints in this car.

The two infallibly distinctive features of the six-cylinder car are the 2.6 badge on the right of the boot lid, and the exhaust peeping out from below the apron with two outlets.

The six-cylinder engine was introduced for the W201 just as the whole Mercedes range was equipped with catalytic converters or prepared, in RÜF form, to receive them. So the 170PS version of the engine that had appeared in the early 260E models was not carried over to the compact saloons. Instead, these were offered with the engine in just two forms, both with a lower (9.2:1) compression ratio than the original. With a catalytic converter installed, the engine's power dropped to 160PS, and in RÜF guise it stood at 166PS.

With a uniquely geared version of the standard five-speed manual gearbox and a 3.27:1 final drive, that was good enough to take a 190E 2.6 to a top speed of 215km/h (133mph), or 212km/h (132mph) in KAT form. The car took 8.2 seconds to accelerate from rest to 100km/h, or 8.5 seconds when fitted with a catalytic converter. The optional automatic gearbox came with a taller 3.07 final drive and peaked at 210km/h (130mph) in RÜF form or 207km/h (128mph) in KAT form. The 100km/h standing-start times for the automatic six-cylinder car were 8.9 seconds

Also new for European markets as a 1987 model was the 190E 2.3, a version of the car that had launched the petrol-engined W201 into the USA. Once again, from most angles it looked exactly like its siblings.

and 9.2 seconds, respectively. Despite optimistic comparisons in some publications of the time (and since), the 190E 2.6 was therefore not as quick as a Cosworth and neither was its top speed as great. Nevertheless, fuel consumption of better than 30mpg (9.4ltr/100km) was achievable, which it was not in the 16-valve car.

Surprisingly, Mercedes made very little effort to distinguish the 2.6 visually from the four-cylinder W201 models. Cosmetic differences were limited to a twin-outlet exhaust tailpipe, a discreet '2.6' badge on the boot lid and a different front apron. Perhaps designed primarily to suit the structural alterations at the front of the car, this had wider air vents than the four-cylinder type and a steeper angle. Power-assisted steering was standard – it was needed because of the extra engine weight over the front wheels – and central locking was also made standard. It was an acknowledgement that this was the flagship of the 201 range.

All this perhaps discouraged potential buyers from seeing the car as a more sporting W201 and rather as a compact luxury saloon; as a result, there was a strong take-up rate for the automatic gearbox model. If Mercedes really had intended it as a foil to the BMW 325i, then the 2.6 missed its mark, because the 325i was always seen as a sporting saloon whereas the six-cylinder Mercedes was not. With hindsight, it seems probable that the 325i was not really the

target at all, although it must have given some impetus to the six-cylinder W201 project.

The first production examples of the 190E 2.6 left the factory in April 1986. The majority must have gone for export, because the six-cylinder car was not launched in Germany until September, which made it a 1987 model. At that point, the price on the car's home market had risen quite dramatically, from the DM39,102 suggested in 1985 to DM44,289. Right-hand-drive models followed after about a year, with the first ones reaching showrooms in Britain during March 1987.

Press Reaction to the 190E 2.6

Even though the six-cylinder W201 would not go on sale in Britain until March 1987, *Autocar* was able to carry out a test drive at its introduction in Germany the previous autumn. The main focus of the report in its issue of 15 October 1986 was on the RÜF cars, because these were the ones that would be coming to Britain. However, a drive in KAT versions also allowed some interesting comparisons between the two.

'It looks very ordinary,' observed *Autocar*, referring to the minimal visual differences between the new car and the existing W201s. The tester was more complimentary about the engine, which benefited from 'the greater urge of an extra two cylinders', was 'quiet on tickover' and 'undoubtedly a fair bit smoother than the four'. Satisfyingly, there were no quirks of handling either: 'Although the switch to the longer and heavier cast-iron block alters the weight distribution this has not affected the 190's generally pleasant road manners.'

The bias was very much towards luxury car rather than sporting model. 'The RUF version… does not feel excessively quick because it is so refined and quiet and the gearing is decidedly "lazy" giving the 190E 2.6 marvellous long-distance and high-speed cruising capability'. The reviewer felt that the automatic version was 'only marginally less responsive', but lamented the KAT model's 'noticeable lack of torque when pulling away from low revs in either fourth or fifth gear'. In his view, the driver should not 'have to work such a large engine to this degree to overcome the strangling effect of the converter'.

Ultimately, the *Autocar* verdict was mixed: 'If what you require is a more refined and comfortable compact saloon than the high-performance 2.3-16 then the newcomer makes a great deal of sense. However, if outright comfort is what you are after the choice would have to be the 260E.' Although the larger car was marginally slower on account of its extra weight, it also cost just £60 more in British showrooms. Buyers tended to agree and, in Britain at least, the six-cylinder W201 would always be a bit-part player.

THE 190E 2.3

Mercedes made sure of grabbing headlines at the 1985 Frankfurt motor show by announcing not only the 190E 2.6 but also a new four-cylinder 190E 2.3. Like the six-cylinder car, however, this would not actually go on sale in Germany until September 1986. It would also be a model that was denied to Britain, as it was to other right-hand-drive markets.

There had of course been a 190E 2.3 model for North America since 1984. The larger-bore version of the M102 engine (as used in the medium-sized 230E models) was necessary to compensate for the power-sapping effects of the emissions-control equipment required by US Federal laws, and to give the entry-level petrol model respectable performance. By 1986, however, Mercedes claimed to have identified a demand for a more powerful four-cylinder 190E outside the USA, and especially in the German domestic market.

The truth, probably, was that they were afraid that the new lower-powered 2.0-litre 190E models in their RÜF and KAT forms for 1986 might persuade buyers to turn towards the BMW 3 Series. By introducing a new model that actually had more power and performance than the original 190E, Mercedes were more than plugging the gap. With 136PS in RÜF form and 132PS in KAT form, the new 190E 2.3 did the job to perfection. There would be no 'continuation' ECE model of the 2.0-litre 190E with its original 122PS specification; the arrival of the 2.3-litre car ensured there was no need for it.

The distinguishing feature of the 2.3-litre model – and there was only one – was the 2.3 badge on the boot lid.

From this angle, it would be impossible to tell what model this is without the helpful number plate applied by the Mercedes press office!

The European 190E 2.3 came with a five-speed manual gearbox as standard or with the established four-speed automatic at extra cost. The five-speed car was claimed to reach 200km/h (124mph) in RÜF form and 197km/h (122mph) when fitted with a catalytic converter. Automatic models were good for 195km/h (121mph) or 192km/h (119mph) in KAT form. These speeds were higher than those that the old, unrestricted 190E had been able to achieve. The 190E 2.3 was very slightly quicker in the 0–100km/h sprint, too. Manual models took 10.3 seconds (or 10.6 seconds in KAT form), and the automatic versions took the same 10.3 seconds in RUF form and 10.7 seconds when fitted with a catalytic converter.

THE 1987 MODELS

If the introduction of models with catalytic converters had been the most important change for the 1986-season W201 range, the 1987 season was characterized by the actual availability of the two new models that had been shown at Frankfurt a year earlier. As a result, there were no fewer than seven variants of the range outside North America. Two were diesels and five had petrol engines. The range was now very comprehensive and arguably more complete than the rather one-sided BMW 3 Series. It included economy models (the 190D), luxury models (the 190E 2.6) and sporting models (the 190E 2.3-16), with several others in between.

There was a new option for 1987 as well, known as ASD. The letters stood for *Automatisches Sperrdifferenzial* ('automatic locking differential'), an electronically controlled system with hydraulic activation that gave varying degrees of differential lock from the standard 15 per cent up to a full 100

THE UK DIM-DIP SYSTEM

New UK lighting regulations that came into force on 1 April 1987 required what was known as a 'dim-dip' headlight system. This caused the dipped headlamps to light up automatically at reduced intensity whenever the side lights were switched on while the engine was running. Side lights could still be used on their own when parking, and the dipped headlamps retained their full intensity when they were needed to illuminate the road at night.

The UK was the only country to introduce such a system, which was its interpretation of a European Directive. However, the European Commission believed that it did not fully meet the aims of the Directive and challenged it in the European Court of Justice. When the court found in favour of the Commission, the UK was forced to amend its lighting regulations.

Mercedes W201 models built for the UK market after October 1986 came with a dim-dip system as standard. However, the system was discontinued in September 1989 when the UK regulations were amended.

190 D 2.5 TURBO

The turbocharged five-cylinder engine out of the car. Here, it is attached to the automatic gearbox that was standard on the first cars.

The new turbocharged five-cylinder engine could be readily identified under the bonnet by the air duct that ran across the top of it. Just visible here is part of the sound-deadening encapsulation on the underside of the bonnet.

Another twin-outlet exhaust and special boot-lid badges marked out the 190D 2.5 Turbo. This example has alloy wheels and rear head restraints as well.

The turbocharged diesel model could also be recognized from the side – as long as it was the
right-hand side. The air-intake vents unique to the model are clearly visible here.

per cent. It was arranged to disengage as soon as the brakes
were applied, so that it did not interfere with the operation of the ABS. When in operation, it alerted the driver by
illuminating an amber warning triangle on the speedometer
face. Its key advantage was that electronic control relieved
the driver of the need to judge when the limited-slip feature
might be needed. In that respect it was a very great improvement on the traditional limited-slip differential, but, like so
many Mercedes options, it was expensive.

Meanwhile, racing versions of the 16-valve car were beginning to make an impression in the DTM (German Touring
Car Championship) (see Chapter 7). For the moment, the
engineers working on the 201 range were able to take a
well-earned rest and focus on future developments – but it
would not be for long.

1988 AND THE 190D 2.5 TURBO

The Mercedes strategy in the US market (see Chapter 6)
depended on big-volume sales of fuel-efficient diesel cars in
order to offset the lower-volume sales of 'gas guzzlers' with
larger engines. This could only work if the company was able

to persuade the Americans of the attraction of diesel power,
and that in turn placed a demand on Stuttgart's engineers
to come up with sufficiently exciting models. One of those
they had developed for the US market was a turbocharged

The air-intake vents on the turbocharged
diesel model in close-up.

Mercedes was proud of its range of turbocharged diesel models, lining them up on the test track at Untertürkheim for this promotional photograph. At the time, the six-cylinder 300D Turbo saloon and 300TD Turbo estate variants of the 124-series range were sold only in North America.

diesel variant of the W201, called the 190D 2.5 Turbo. That car had gone on sale in its intended market in spring 1986.

It was something of a surprise to find a Europeanized 190D 2.5 Turbo on the Mercedes stand at Frankfurt in September 1987, some fifteen months later. By all accounts, it was also a last-minute decision to feature it at the show. Although the car was made available in European markets more or less immediately, it would never be sold in Britain. The official explanation was that the position of the turbocharger made it impossible to engineer the car for right-hand drive. However, most modifications are possible if the will is there, so it is more likely that the market for diesel cars in Britain was still too small to justify the cost of developing a right-hand-drive 190D 2.5 Turbo.

Turbocharged diesel engines were of course nothing new for Mercedes. They had been introduced to the company's commercial vehicles as early as 1953, and in the 1970s a series of experimental cars had led to the development of a turbocharged passenger car engine in the US-market 300SD introduced in 1977. The engine in the 190D 2.5 Turbo was essentially the same 2.5-litre five-cylinder OM602 diesel as in the unblown 190D 2.5. However, the basic design had been re-engineered to take the greater stresses associated with turbocharging, and the OM602 D 25 A engine had several special features. That engine code, by the way, was typical of the detailed types that Mercedes used: the OM602 part needs no explanation; the D 25 indicates a 2.5-litre diesel; and the A stands for *Abgasturbolader*, or 'exhaust-driven turbocharger'.

Specifically, the bottom-end changes to the basic OM602 design consisted of a larger-capacity sump, a bigger oil pump and a hardened crankshaft running in uprated bearings. At the top end, there were different pistons that were cooled by jets of oil and had special rings and gudgeon pins; the pre-chambers were also modified; and the exhaust valves were filled with sodium to aid cooling. The turbocharger itself was mounted on the right (exhaust) side of the engine, with an air duct that ran across the valve cover to the inlet manifold on the other side. It was made by Mercedes' usual supplier, the Garrett corporation in the USA, and delivered a maximum boost of 13psi from around 2,000rpm.

The location of the turbocharger created a challenge in that it had to be close to the air intake and filter. To ensure that there was enough airflow, the Mercedes engineers provided a set of six inlet slots in the right-hand front wing between the turn indicator lens and the wheel arch. This would always be a distinctive feature of the turbocharged W201, which was otherwise recognizable only by a '2.5 Turbo' badge on the boot lid and by the twin exhaust tailpipes peeping out from below the rear bumper apron.

With 122PS in European guise, the 190D 2.5 Turbo came only with an automatic gearbox. Performance was similar to that of the 2.0-litre petrol 190E, which was no mean feat for a diesel saloon in the 1980s. A tall 2.65:1 axle ratio allowed the car a top speed of 192km/h (119mph), and the 0–100km/h sprint could be despatched in 11.5 seconds. Fuel consumption averaged around 37.6mpg (7.6ltr/100km), which was excellent, but of course was offset by the car's

INTERIOR COLOURS FOR W201 MODELS, 1986–1988

Upholstery was available in Cloth, MB-Tex, Velour or Leather. There were eight colours for 1986, which were Black, Blue, Brazil, Dark Olive, Date, Cream Beige, Grey and Mid Red. Pine Green replaced Dark Olive from June 1986. Note that Velour never came in Black, but in Anthracite.

high initial cost. At DM43,719 before extras in Germany on its release, the 190D 2.5 Turbo was approaching the showroom price of a 190E 2.6 and never became a very strong seller, despite its undoubted qualities.

The European 190D 2.5 Turbo was on sale in its original form for just a year. In autumn 1988, it was facelifted in the same way as all the other models of the W201 range (*see* Chapter 4 for details).

Paint Colours for W201 models, 1986–1988

German name	English name	Code	Model-year		
			1986	1987	1988
Beige					
Hellelfenbein	Taxi Beige/Light Ivory	623	✓	✓	✓
Pueblobeige	Pueblo Beige	651	✓	✓	✓
Black					
Schwarz	Black	040	✓	✓	✓
Blue					
Diamantblau	Diamond Blue metallic	355	✓	✓	✓
Dunkelblau	Midnight Blue	904	✓	✓	✓
Nautikblau	Nautical Blue metallic	929	✓	✓	✓
Petrol	Blue-Green metallic	877	✓	✓	✓
Surfblau	Surf Blue	900	✓	✓	✓
Brown					
Bisonbraun	Havana Brown metallic	432	✓	✓	✓
Champagner	Champagne metallic	473	✓	✓	
Impala	Impala Brown metallic	441	✓	✓	✓
Maroonbraun	Maroon Brown	459	✓		
Green					
Achatgrün	Agate Green	815	✓	✓	✓
Nachtgrün	Pine Green metallic	254	✓	✓	✓
Nelkengrün	Willow Green metallic	261	✓	✓	✓
Grey					
Anthrazitgrau	Anthracite Grey metallic	172	✓	✓	✓
Blauschwarz	Blue-Black metallic	199	✓	✓	✓
Liasgrau	Ascot Grey	751	✓	✓	✓
Perlmuttgrau	Pearl Grey metallic	122	✓	✓	✓
Red					
Barolorot	Barolo Red	540	✓	✓	✓
Pajettrot	Pajett Red metallic	587	✓	✓	✓
Signalrot	Signal Red	568	✓	✓	✓
Silver					
Astralsilber	Astral Silver metallic	735	✓	✓	✓
Rauchsilber	Smoke Silver	702	✓	✓	✓
White					
Arcticweiss	Arctic White	147	✓	✓	✓
Yellow					
Hellocker	Light Ochre	690	✓		

Note: Rauchsilber was available only on the 190E 2.3-16.

TECHNICAL SPECIFICATIONS: MERCEDES-BENZ W201 MODELS, 1986–1988 MODEL-YEARS

Engine (190)

M102 four-cylinder with cast-iron block and alloy cylinder head
1997cc (89mm bore × 80.25mm stroke)
Single overhead camshaft, two valves per cylinder
Five-bearing crankshaft

ECE version
Compression ratio 9.1:1
Stromberg 175 CDT carburettor
Max. power 105PS at 5,200rpm
Max. torque 170Nm at 2,500rpm

RÜF version
Compression ratio 9.1:1
Pierburg 2E-E carburettor with electronic control
Max. power 105PS at 5,500rpm
Max. torque 165Nm at 3,000rpm

KAT version
Compression ratio 9.1:1
Pierburg 2E-E carburettor with electronic control
Max. power 102PS at 5,500rpm
Max. torque 160Nm at 3,000rpm

Engine (190E)

M102E four-cylinder with cast-iron block and alloy cylinder head
1997cc (89mm bore × 80.25mm stroke)
Single overhead camshaft, two valves per cylinder
Five-bearing crankshaft

ECE version
Compression ratio 9.1:1
Bosch KE-Jetronic mechanical fuel injection
Max. power 122PS at 5,100rpm
Max. torque 178Nm at 3,500rpm

KAT version
Compression ratio 9.1:1
Bosch KE-Jetronic mechanical fuel injection

Max. power 118PS at 5,100rpm
Max. torque 172Nm at 3,500rpm

Engine (190E 2.3)

M102 four-cylinder with cast-iron block and alloy cylinder head
2299cc (95.5mm bore × 80.25mm stroke)
Single overhead camshaft, two valves per cylinder
Five-bearing crankshaft

RÜF version
Compression ratio 9.0:1
Bosch KE-Jetronic mechanical fuel injection
Max. power 136PS at 5,100rpm
Max. torque 205Nm at 3,500rpm

KAT version
Compression ratio 9.0:1
Bosch KE-Jetronic mechanical fuel injection
Max. power 132PS at 5,100rpm
Max. torque 198Nm at 3,500rpm

Engine (190E 2.3-16)

M102 four-cylinder with cast-iron block and alloy cylinder head
2299cc (95mm bore × 80.25mm stroke)
Two overhead camshafts, four valves per cylinder
Five-bearing crankshaft

ECE version
Compression ratio 10.5:1
Bosch KE-Jetronic mechanical fuel injection
Max. power 185PS at 6,200rpm
Max. torque 235Nm at 4,500rpm

RÜF version
Compression ratio 9.7:1
Bosch KE-Jetronic mechanical fuel injection
Max. power 177PS at 5,800rpm
Max. torque 230Nm at 4,750rpm

KAT version
Compression ratio 9.7:1
Bosch KE-Jetronic mechanical fuel injection
Max. power 170PS at 5,800rpm
Max. torque 220Nm at 4,750rpm

Engine (190E 2.6)
M103 six-cylinder with cast-iron block and alloy cylinder
  head
2599cc (82.9mm bore × 80.25mm stroke)
Single overhead camshaft, two valves per cylinder
Four-bearing crankshaft

RÜF version
Compression ratio 9.2:1
Bosch KE-Jetronic mechanical fuel injection
Max. power 166PS at 5,800rpm
Max. torque 228Nm at 4,600rpm

KAT version
Compression ratio 9.2:1
Bosch KE-Jetronic mechanical fuel injection
Max. power 160PS at 5,800rpm
Max. torque 220Nm at 4,600rpm

Engine (190D)
OM601 four-cylinder diesel with cast-iron block and alloy
  cylinder head
1997cc (87mm bore × 84mm stroke)
Single overhead camshaft, two valves per cylinder
Five-bearing crankshaft
Compression ratio 22:1
Indirect injection with Bosch pump
Max. power 72PS at 4,600rpm
Max. torque 123Nm at 2,800rpm

Engine (190D 2.5)
OM602 five-cylinder with cast-iron block and alloy cylinder
  head
2497cc (87mm bore × 84mm stroke)
Single overhead camshaft, two valves per cylinder
Six-bearing crankshaft
Compression ratio 22:1
Indirect injection with Bosch pump
Max. power 90PS at 4,600rpm
Max. torque 154Nm at 2,800rpm

Engine (190D 2.5 Turbo)
OM602 five-cylinder with cast-iron block and alloy cylinder
  head
2497cc (87mm bore × 84mm stroke)

Single overhead camshaft, two valves per cylinder
Six-bearing crankshaft
Compression ratio 22:1
Indirect injection with Bosch pump and Garrett T-25
  turbocharger
Max. power 122PS at 4,600rpm
Max. torque 225Nm at 2,400rpm

Gearbox
Four-speed manual GL68/20 G (190, 190E)
  Ratios 3.91:1, 2.17:1, 1.37:1, 1.00:1, reverse 3.78:1
Four-speed manual GL68/20 D (190D)
  Ratios 4.23:1, 2.36:1, 1.49:1, 1.00:1, reverse 4.10:1
Five-speed manual GL68/20 B-5 (190, 190E, 190E 2.3, 190D
from November 1985, 190D 2.5)
  Ratios 3.91:1, 2.17:1, 1.37:1, 1.00:1, 0.78:1, reverse 4.27:1
Five-speed manual GL68/20 A-5 (190D to October 1985)
  Ratios 4.23:1, 2.36:1, 1.49:1, 1.00:1, 0.84:1, reverse 4.63:1
Five-speed manual GL76/27 F-5 (190E 2.6)
  Ratios 3.86:1, 2.18:1, 1.38:1, 1.00:1, 0.80:1, reverse 4.22:1
Five-speed close-ratio manual (190E 2.3-16)
  Ratios 4.08:1, 2.52:1, 1.77:1, 1.26:1, 1.00:1, reverse 4.16:1
Four-speed automatic W4A 020 (190, 190E, 190E 2.3, 190E
2.3-16, 190E 2.6, 190D, 190D 2.5, 190D 2.5 Turbo)
  Ratios 4.25:1, 2.41:1, 1.49:1, 1.00:1, reverse 5.67:1

Axle ratio
2.65:1 (190D 2.5 Turbo)
3.07:1 (190E 2.3-16 ECE models, 190E 2.6 automatic, 190D
  2.5 automatic)
3.23:1 (190, 190E, 190D)
3.27:1 (190E 2.3, 190E 2.3-16 RÜF and KAT models, 190E
  2.6 five-speed)
3.64:1 (190D 2.5 five-speed)
3.91:1 (190D five-speed from November 1985)

Suspension
Front suspension with MacPherson struts, wishbones, coil
  springs, telescopic gas dampers and anti-roll bar; adjustable
  ride height optional on 190E 2.3-16.
Rear suspension with five links, coil springs, telescopic gas
  dampers and anti-roll bar; hydro-pneumatic self-levelling
  strut standard on 190E 2.3-16 and optional on other
  models.

Steering
Recirculating-ball steering with power assistance.

Brakes
Disc brakes on all four wheels, ventilated at the front on 190E 2.3-16 and 190E 2.6; dual hydraulic circuit and servo assistance; ABS optional (standard on 190E 2.3-16 and 190E 2.6).

Dimensions
Overall length: 4,420mm (4,430mm for 190E 2.3-16)
Overall width: 1,678 mm (1,706mm for 190E 2.3-16)
Overall height: 1,390mm
   1,361mm for 190E 2.3-16
Wheelbase: 2,665mm
Track, front: 1,428mm to December 1984
   1,437mm from January 1985
   1,445mm for 190E 2.3-16

Track, rear: 1,415mm to December 1984
   1,418mm from January 1985
   1,429mm for 190E 2.3-16

Wheels and tyres
6J × 15 steel disc wheels with 185/65 R 15 tyres
6J × 15 alloy wheels with 185/65 R 15 tyres optional
7J × 15 alloy wheels with 205/55 VR 15 tyres, for 190E 2.3-16

Running weight
190: 1,130kg
190E: 1,140kg
190E 2.3: 1,190kg
190E 2.3-16: 1,260kg
190E 2.6: 1,220kg
190D: 1,140kg
190D 2.5: 1,175kg
190D 2.5 Turbo: 1,250kg

CHAPTER FOUR

A BUSY TIME:
THE 1989–1990 MODEL-YEARS

With all the mainstream variants of the W201 now firmly in place, Mercedes could move on to the next stage of the range's life, which was the planned mid-life facelift. Outside North America, there were now eight W201 models. Three were diesels – the 190D, 190D 2.5 and 190D 2.5 Turbo – and five had petrol engines – the 190, 190E, 190E 2.3, 190E 2.6 and the 16-valve Cosworth car. All of these would remain in production for the next couple of years, although the Cosworth car became a 190E 2.5-16 for 1989, and it would be supplemented by two limited-production homologation specials that were needed to support Mercedes' efforts in touring car racing (see Chapter 7 for more on that story).

The mid-life facelift really did occur more or less at the mid-point of the 201's production run, as it was announced in September 1988 at the Paris motor show. By that time, the cars had been in production for just under six years; although Mercedes were not about to disclose such information at that stage, it would be a further five years before the range was replaced.

THE 1989 MODEL-YEAR FACELIFT

The cars introduced at the Paris Salon in September 1988 as 1989 models were readily distinguishable from those that had gone before. Most obviously, they all had plastic lower flank panels; broadly similar to those on the Cosworth cars,

The mid-life facelift for 1989 brought plastic flank panels that were broadly similar to those on the 16-valve cars. Colour matches with the paintwork were usually close, but were not always exact. Still very recognizably W201 types, the 1989 models had nevertheless taken on the appearance of a larger car.

these had the key purpose of improving resistance to minor damage and reducing the risk of rust in the doors. Less immediately obvious was the passenger's door mirror now being fitted as standard on all models.

The bumpers had been redesigned with new mountings and were claimed to be capable of withstanding greater impacts than before. At the front, they were covered by a new apron that took its design from the one used on the first 190E 2.6 models. The theory was that this reduced front axle lift and improved high-speed handling, although in both cases these benefits really applied only to the fastest models. There was a deeper rear apron as well.

Modellpflege '88 Baureihe 201

The German term for a facelift is *Mopf*, an abbreviation of the word *Modellpflege* seen on this promotional cutaway drawing. The car is clearly a carburettor 190, a model that would remain available only until the end of the 1990 calendar-year.

MERCEDES-BENZ UNFALLVERSUCH

Mercedes claimed that the offset frontal crash test represented the most common type of collision. Although the basic W201 structure had been crash-tested several times before, examples with the latest plastic side cladding were also slammed into concrete walls, to make sure there was no deterioration in their crashworthiness.

The new flank panels and aprons were certainly distinctive, but they were not an unqualified success. Undeniably, they gave more of a 'big car' look to the range, which was, of course, just as compact as ever. However, it is also arguable that they made the W201 models appear heavier and less graceful than before – especially when the standard steel wheels were fitted. Despite Mercedes' claim that improvements in the impregnation process had now made a wider colour range possible, there clearly remained some limitations. In some cases, the colour matching of plastic to paint was very approximate, giving some cars a two-tone effect that was not entirely pleasing.

The interior changes were perhaps more worthwhile. Mercedes had moved the rear seat cross-member to give an extra 0.8in legroom and 0.2in headroom for rear-seat passengers. The seats themselves had mean-while been quite radically modified, with foam construction (as in the mid-sized W124 models) instead of sprung steel. The rear seat, never really wide enough for three, changed from a bench type to one with two individually shaped seats. A range of brighter and more attractive upholstery fabrics replaced the rather sombre earlier selection. The centre console was also modified to resemble that in the 124 range and to reinforce that 'big car' feel.

Lower axle ratios on several models improved acceleration, although inevitably they were accompanied by a small increase in fuel consumption. At a time when German cars

The dashboard was not altered at the time of the facelift in autumn 1988, although there were changes to the interior fabrics and colours, and of course to the seats themselves.

generally were suffering from worse fuel consumption because of the introduction of catalytic converters, Mercedes had clearly calculated that they could get away with this. For those who were really concerned – and probably very few customers were – the 70-litre fuel tank from the 16-valve cars became available as an optional alternative to the standard 55-litre size. Presumably reflecting customer demand, the 190D 2.5 Turbo for 1989 had a five-speed manual gearbox as standard, and the automatic that had earlier been standard was now relegated to an extra-cost option.

Top models in the facelifted range were the new 190E 2.5-16, seen here on the left, and the 190E 2.6.

THE 190E 2.5-16

The only really new model unveiled at Frankfurt in September 1988 was a revised version of the 16-valve car. Reflecting its new and larger engine, this was badged as a 190E 2.5-16, and its announcement was accompanied by news that Mercedes would now be giving official support to teams competing in the DTM (German Touring Car Championship).

The new model, however, was not really a homologation special in the way that its 2.3-litre predecessor had been;

instead, it was more of a response to the roadgoing BMW M3, which boasted 200PS as against the 185PS of the 2.3-litre Cosworth Mercedes. The increase in engine capacity was also just a stage on the way to the proper homologation special, which would be revealed at the Geneva motor show in March 1989. For the moment, the car that was offered to the public was simply an improved and uprated version of the car they had been offered earlier.

The new 2.5-litre engine was a further development of the earlier 2.3-litre type. As well as a longer stroke and lighter pistons, it also had a dual-row timing chain instead of the single-row type in the earlier engine, which had tended to give trouble. The cylinder head was still cast by Cosworth – in this guise it was known to its British manufacturer as the WAB type – but there was a noticeable absence of references to Cosworth in publicity for the new car. This was no doubt because Cosworth had also worked with Ford to develop the Ford Sierra Cosworth, which was now challenging the Mercedes entries in the DTM races!

The new car had 204PS at 6,750rpm in RUF form. Although this dropped to 195PS when a catalytic converter was fitted, both figures were usefully higher than the 185PS of the 2.3-litre car. With taller gearing than before, the 190E 2.5-16 was capable of 150mph (241km/h) and could despatch the 0–60mph sprint in 7.7 seconds. It also came in two colours that had not been available on the earlier car: Almandine Red and Astral Silver. Blue-Black metallic and Smoke Silver remained available, and for 1990 Brilliant Silver would replace Astral Silver as an option. The new 2.5-litre car also came with ASD as standard in place of the limited-slip differential of the 2.3-litre cars.

The new version of the 16-valve car came with new colours, to distinguish it more readily from the earlier 2.3-litre version. One of them was Almandine Red, seen here.

The new red colour option certainly suited the 16-valve car, which from this angle would otherwise have been impossible to distinguish from the older model.

Tail badges came to the rescue again, although it was not easy to distinguish those
of the 2.5-litre model from those of the 2.3-litre car at a distance.

EVOLUTION

One factor that limited further development of the Cosworth models as track racers was their engine configuration. The original 16-valve engine had been based on the
existing 2.3-litre four-cylinder M102, which had a relatively
long stroke. This would have been fine for the original concept of a rally car, but the DTM track cars needed to rev
very high to achieve competitive speeds. The long stroke
hindered this, so the only solution was to redevelop the
engine with a shorter stroke.

The DTM regulations permitted the use of an 'evolution'
variant of the car originally homologated, on condition that
at least 10 per cent of the road car equivalents were built
with the same evolutionary components. As homologation
called for 5,000 cars, that meant that there would have to be
at least 500 examples of any new variant. Production totals
of the original car could be counted towards the 5,000, so
Mercedes was allowed to count production of the original
190E 2.3-16 when calculating its numbers.

Under the bonnet, there was not a lot to distinguish
the new engine from the old one, either!

The 16-valve 2.5-litre car was only a stepping stone towards the homologation special that was created to enable improvements to the **DTM** racers. Looking very much the part, the Evolution was released as a limited edition. Its lower stance, new front apron, widened arches and larger wheels were ready recognition features.

The Evolution always came in **Blue-Black metallic**, which looked grey in some lights
– as it did at this classic car show in Berlin. MATTI BLUME/WIKIMEDIA COMMONS

The plan that emerged was to develop a short-stroke 2.5-litre engine that could be used as the basis of a much more highly developed race engine for the DTM cars. The engineers re-worked the M102 16-valve engine with a shorter stroke and a larger bore, which gave an overall swept volume slightly below that of the standard 2.5-16 engine. Cosworth developed a further revised cylinder head, which they knew as the WAC type. There were further changes that improved the engine's tuneability and its ability to run at sustained high revs. Lighter pistons reduced the weight of the rotating mass, the lubrication system was uprated, and the cam timing was altered.

Other changes were dialled in to assist development of the DTM racers. Racing regulations allowed wheels to be no more than 2 inches larger in diameter than those on the equivalent road cars; the existing road cars had 15-inch wheels, so Mercedes decided to give the Evolution model 16-inch wheels. These would give room for larger brakes on the track cars, among other things. There was also a quicker steering ratio, giving 2.7 turns of the wheel from lock to lock instead of the three turns needed on the standard cars.

The roadgoing version of the revised car was announced at the Geneva show in March 1989 as the 190E 2.5-16 Evolution. There were to be 500 cars for sale to the public, although in practice 502 examples would be built; the required number had been built by May 1989, which allowed the new short-stroke engine to go racing in the DTM. All the road cars had left-hand drive and all were finished in Blue-Black metallic paint. They were dressed to look the part, too, with a noticeably lower ride height than the standard production models and with wheel-arch extensions to cover fat 205/55 tyres on wider wheel rims. There was also a taller spoiler on the boot lid and, less visibly, there were larger brakes with 300mm ventilated front discs and 278mm rear discs; on the standard 2.5-16, the brakes were all solid discs, with a 284mm diameter at the front and a 258mm diameter at the rear. The cars all had three-stage height adjustment for the front suspension, controlled from the dashboard and intended to improve high-speed aerodynamics.

Yet there was little hint of the engine's potential in the specification it had on these cars. Mercedes claimed its power and torque figures were identical to those of the standard 190E 2.5-16. A lower final drive ratio kept acceleration figures similar, and perhaps the only mechanical concession

to the image of a high-performance car was that no automatic gearbox option was listed. However, for those customers who insisted on some extra performance, tuning specialists AMG (which ran one of the works teams in the DTM) made available an optional Power Pack. Priced at DM 18,000, this boosted power to 235PS at 7,200rpm through altered camshafts, a larger-diameter throttle body, changes to the inlet and exhaust systems, and a modified engine control system. Torque meanwhile increased to 245Nm at 5,000rpm. The top speed was claimed to be 250km/h (155mph), which was the maximum for a road car under the agreement among German manufacturers.

These cars would later become known as the Evo I or Evolution I models, after a further-developed Evolution II model was introduced in 1990. They were always formidably expensive: DM87,204.30 in West Germany on their introduction, while the standard 2.5-16 was DM69,084. Although none were built with right-hand drive, the cars were certainly available to special order in right-hand-drive countries such as Britain, although they would understandably always be very rare.

DIESEL POWER

The Geneva show in 1989 was also the occasion when Mercedes introduced some changes for its diesel-engined W201 models. A slight peak power increase for the 190D 2.5 Turbo (from 122PS to 126PS) had gone almost unnoticed at Frankfurt in September 1988. The explanation came in February 1989, when Mercedes research scientist Dr Manfred Fortnagel presented a paper that outlined a new way of reducing particle emissions from indirect-injection diesel engines. With that reduction in particle emissions came a modified injection pump that also delivered a little more power. The 190D 2.5 Turbo had already benefited from it, and now the new technology would be applied to Mercedes' other diesel engines.

For the W201, that meant changes to the four-cylinder engine in the 190D and to the five-cylinder in the naturally aspirated 190D 2.5. So from March 1989, the 190D went from 72PS to 75PS and the 190D 2.5 went from 90PS to 94PS. The changes were barely noticeable in everyday driving, even though they looked good on paper, but at least Mercedes were keeping on the right side of the West German government by making progress to reduce air pollution.

A late 1989 model with the Sportline option: the lowered ride height is not immediately obvious, but the small Sportline badge let into the cladding on the front wing can be seen.

SPORTLINE

Mercedes' decision to give factory support to teams racing the Cosworth cars in the DTM for 1989, and its introduction of the 2.5-litre Cosworth car and the subsequent Evolution special edition, were all indications that the company had recognized a need to improve its sporting credentials. Stuttgart planned to take the fight to the enemy, which at the time was clearly identified as BMW.

The next stage in improving Mercedes' sporting image was reached in June 1989, with the introduction of the Sportline range. Available as an option on all W201 models except the Cosworth and the Evolution, Sportline affected not only the cars' handling but also their interior ambiance. On the handling side, Sportline brought suspension lowered by

23mm, with stiffer springs and dampers, 7J x 15 alloy wheels and wider 205/55 R 15 tyres. The steering was sharpened up, too. The interior of Sportline-equipped W201s came with the seating package from the Cosworth cars, plus a leather shift lever gaiter and a leather-covered gear knob bearing the Sportline emblem. There was also a leather-bound steering wheel with a 390mm diameter in place of the standard 400mm size, which helped increase the apparent weight of the steering and also gave a welcome improvement in thigh room for the driver.

When the Sportline option was ordered, it was always accompanied by a small identifying badge on the flank panel just behind each front wheel arch. Mercedes saw the Sportline package as an important weapon in the fight against the more overtly sporting BMW 3 Series, and insisted that it sold very well. In Britain, however, the take-up rate was disappointingly low. Perhaps the main reason was because Mercedes W201 customers were for the most part quite happy with the cars as they were.

The Mercedes-Benz Sportline package
You won't know
what's in it until you open it up

This English-language sales leaflet for the Sportline package had a superb strapline: 'You won't know what it is until you open it up.' MAGIC CAR PICS

An Evolution II being sold through All Time Stars, the sales division of Mercedes-Benz Classic. Even more extreme visually, all these cars had a large Evolution badge on the front wing, at the rear of the wheel-arch blister.

Six-spoke wheels, wheel-arch blisters and that outrageous rear spoiler were all recognition features of the Evolution II. This was the car that homologated features that would eventually produce a DTM-winning car for Mercedes.

Disappointingly, perhaps, the engine of the Evolution II was a standard roadgoing 2.5-16 type, although it was enhanced by the AMG Performance Pack that had been an option on the earlier Evolution. The red plug leads were not a standard feature. TKOSHO24V/WIKIMEDIA COMMONS

THE 1990 MODELS

There was clearly a focus on Mercedes' 'performance' programme at the Frankfurt show in September 1989, when Sportline was promoted as just one element in the new challenge to BMW. However, it is important to recognize that Mercedes had not decided to re-position themselves as

direct competitors to BMW on all levels; their strategy was more cautious than that. The traditional Mercedes approach was still very evident in most models, but over the next few years there would be more sporting options available, whether as enhancements of standard cars (such as Sport-line) or as standalone models.

As a result, the headline new car at Frankfurt in 1989 was a high-performance 24-valve variant of the top-model W124 saloon that bore 300E-24 badges. Just a year later, the high-performance V8-engined 500E variant of the W124 saloons took the battle a stage further by challenging the established BMW M5. The W201 range already had its BMW challenger in the Cosworth models, and later in the season another new special-edition variant would help to make clear how seriously Stuttgart was taking the fight.

For the W201s at Frankfurt in 1989, however, the changes were limited. Mercedes focused on gearing modifications that would improve accelerative performance across the range, although the close-ratio Getrag five-speed gearbox in the Cosworth models was not affected. The carburettor 190 took on the 190E's four-speed manual gearbox with its lower intermediate ratios; internal ratios were made common between the four-speed and five-speed gearboxes in most cases, and there was a taller overdrive fifth gear for the 190D 2.5. The 190E 2.6, meanwhile, took on a lower axle ratio to improve its acceleration.

Less exciting, perhaps, but no less important as far as Mercedes were concerned, was the fact that the 1990-model cars announced at Frankfurt all came with catalytic

Instruments in the Evolution II were the same as in the standard road car, with a stopwatch (some called it a lap timer) in the lower console. MAGIC CAR PICS

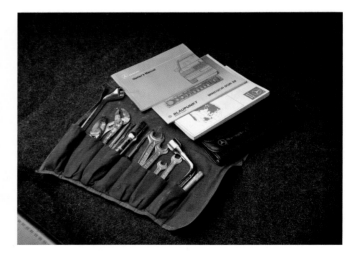

This kit of small tools was a rather attractive extra that came with the Evolution II. MAGIC CAR PICS

converters as standard. The last of the old ECE specification models disappeared, as did the RÜF cars, with their half-and-half specification. It all made for simplification on the production lines and (at least in the eyes of the West German government) for cleaner air as well.

THE EVOLUTION II

The racing versions of the Evolution cars improved Mercedes' performance on the DTM tracks, but they were certainly not the cure-all that the company might have been hoping for – not least because BMW had also raised their game with the latest versions of the M3. Before the end of the 1989 racing season it was quite obvious that something more was needed if Mercedes seriously wanted to challenge for the championship. The company sought that something more by visiting Professor Richard Eppler, an aerodynamics specialist based at the University of Stuttgart.

In conjunction with the Mercedes engineers, Eppler came up with a bodykit of adjustable wings and spoilers that was like nothing else ever seen on a Mercedes. In order to homologate it for racing, Mercedes were obliged once again to build a minimum of 500 examples. By the time of the Geneva show, in March 1990, they had a new special-edition W201 ready for sale: the 190E 2.5-16 Evolution II.

There was no doubt that the Evo II had a stunning presence and the bodykit was radical by any standards, let alone those of a conservative manufacturer like Mercedes. According to *Mercedes Enthusiast* magazine in February 2009, 'Even when you know what it is, it's still hard to compute that this is a genuine product from Mercedes, and not the result of a boy racer's vivid imagination.'

Its most striking element was a huge adjustable spoiler mounted on the boot lid, with a fixed upper wing and an adjustable lower one. This was matched at the front by a precariously low splitter on the air dam that could be moved forwards by an inch on its mountings to improve the downforce on the front wheels at speed. There were also streamlined wheel-arch 'blisters' to cover the wider tracks, and at the rear a special rear apron was needed to blend these into the lines of the bodywork.

Noticeable only from behind was a plastic cover over the top of the rear window, which has often been misunderstood as a further aerodynamic feature. It was in fact nothing of the sort. The DTM regulations stated that any rear spoiler must not interfere with the driver's view out of the rear of the car, and of course the huge top wing of the Evolution II would have done exactly that. The Mercedes solution – and it was a cheeky one – was to fit that cover over the window so that the wing could not be seen in the rear view mirror. It met the letter of the regulations, if not perhaps their spirit.

At the high speeds of which the racing Mercedes were capable, the bodykit had the very useful benefit of increasing downforce, to the benefit of traction and handling. In combination with the other changes to the car (of which more in a moment), it lowered the drag coefficient to 0.29 from the standard W201's 0.33, as demonstrated by tests in a wind tunnel. Realistically, however, its main benefit for the roadgoing versions of the Evo II was that it made them utterly unmistakeable, thus giving them a very special kudos.

Like the earlier Evolution model, the Evo II came with height-adjustable front and rear suspension, which was certainly valuable in helping to protect that vulnerable front apron. It had unique six-spoke alloy wheels made by Speedline, which had a 17-inch diameter that under DTM regulations allowed the racers to run wheels of up to 19 inches in diameter. The tyres specified when the cars were new were Dunlop SP Sport D40 M2 types with a size of 245/40 ZR 17.

As for the engine, it was the same short-stroke 2.5-litre as in the earlier Evolution models, but this time with the AMG Power Pack as standard. As a result, the power output of all Evo II models was 235PS at 7,200rpm, although the engine's rev limit was a high 7,800rpm. Unsurprisingly, the only gearbox option was the close-ratio Getrag five-speed with its dog's-leg gate, and once again the car was electronically limited to the 250km/h agreed as a maximum for roadgoing cars among German manufacturers.

There are various stories associated with the launch of the Evo II at Geneva. Some suggest that all 500 examples had been sold before the car was officially announced; others claim that all 500 were sold within a week. One way or the other, Mercedes scrambled to build them. The full 500 had been completed by the end of April and the Evo II was homologated for racing on 1 May 1990. It made its first appearance on the race tracks in June.

All 500 production models of the Evo II were delivered in Blue-Black metallic paint, exactly as on the earlier Evolution cars. However, and again as with the earlier Evolution, there were actually 502 cars built. The last two, numbers 501 and 502, were painted in Astral Silver; one went to Mercedes-

COMPARING THE COSWORTHS

In the May 2007 issue of *Mercedes Enthusiast* magazine, writer James Mills gathered together an example of each roadgoing Cosworth Mercedes for a comparison test. The 190E 2.3-16 was, slightly unusually, an automatic-gearbox model. Unsurprisingly, it was the least exciting performer of all. 'All the more remarkable,' wrote Mills, 'is how together its underpinnings feel on the road. Although the 2299cc motor is down on power in this company – exacerbated by this car's autobox – the chassis makes up for it with a sure-footed, grippy stance and a precision that instils immediate confidence. Knocking the gear lever back into third, you can keep the twin-cam 16-valve motor revving away in its natural sweet spot – above 4000rpm – and marvel at the chassis' composure.'

Mills used his own 190E 2.5-16 to represent the later 'standard' models. 'It makes the 2.3-16 feel like it was being strangled by an unseen pair of sinister hands,' he wrote. 'The revs come more freely, throttle response feels sharper, speed builds more rapidly and the 7000rpm redline is more regularly encountered. Suddenly, we're dealing with a car that feels properly rapid.'

He also had some pertinent views on the much-maligned gate of the Getrag gearbox: 'The dog's-leg Getrag is absolutely wonderful – if you forget all about first gear… The trick to the manual is to rely on second gear as much as possible, or shift out of first once you're rolling. From there, second to third and fourth to fifth are a rapid-fire delight.'

As for the Evo I, 'The car sits flatter than the standard 2.5 and rides the lumps and bumps better with its tighter suspension set up, refusing to get flustered even at silly speeds. But you need more commitment to get the best from it, the wider wheels and tyres clinging to the tarmac for longer and the tail staying more resolutely planted. The steering is an improvement as well, with sharper responses…. And the 300mm brakes are unquestionably a step in the right direction. [But the performance] comes as a bit of a letdown. The only real gain is right at the top of the rev range – perfect for track driving.'

The Evo II was less than fully evaluated this time around, but for the magazine's February 2009 issue Mills was able to borrow another one. Of this, he commented that 'the motor surprises you with its smooth and civilized idle, and it revs freely as you blip the throttle'. He went on to elaborate: 'That is the irony: from the way it looks you are led to expect a hot-headed raging bull of a car, but beneath the surface it is still a Mercedes-Benz through and through.' Still on the theme of the car's character being quite different from expectations, he added that 'the level of comfort served up by the suspension is more than passable…. [It] smothers out imperfections on any typical B-road, remaining taut and flat as you feed in the steering and switch direction.'

The 16-valve cars line up for the camera: (back) an original 2.3-litre model; (centre) the first 2.5-litre Evolution model; and (foreground) an Evolution II. All are painted Blue-Black metallic.

This 1991 model for the UK market shows how well dark colours suited the W201.

Benz for their museum and the other went to AMG, which was running the DTM racing programme. The cars were massively expensive when announced in March 1989, with a price tag of DM104,440 in their native Germany at a time when a 190E cost less than DM40,000. All of them of course had left-hand drive but, as before, it was possible to buy one as a special order in Britain, where they cost £55,000 each.

LAST, BUT NOT LEAST: THE 190E 1.8

An Injected Engine

The relentless march of emissions-control legislation around the world had persuaded Mercedes to use electronically controlled injection systems for more and more of its cars. As a result, the W201 190 was the very last petrol-engined model to be fuelled by a carburettor. It was still selling well by 1990 but Mercedes had plans to replace it with a model that had an injected engine, which could be more easily tuned to meet changing emissions requirements.

The new engine was once again a variant of the M102 four-cylinder, and it broke new ground for Mercedes in having a capacity of less than a nominal 2 litres. Not since the 180 Ponton models of the early- and mid-1950s had such a small petrol engine been available, and it may be that its basic design dated from the time when the W201 was being designed and Mercedes had considered sub-2.0-litre engines. Its 89mm bore was the same as that in the 2-litre M102 types, but its shorter stroke of 72.2mm brought the swept volume down to just 1797cc. To reduce internal losses, the Mercedes engineers designed its new crankshaft without a vibration damper, and with only four counter-weights instead of the eight used to smooth out the other M102 engines.

It was a measure of the advances made in engine efficiency over the last decade that the injected 1.8-litre engine, delivered 109PS at 5,500rpm, while the carburettor 2.0-litre in the 190 that it would eventually replace was rated at,105PS at 5,700rpm. The shorter stroke nevertheless made,for rather less torque, which peaked with 150Nm at 3,500rpm; the carburettor car developed 158Nm at the same crankshaft speed. Maximum speed was slightly higher, the new model reaching 185km/h (115mph) as compared with the 183km/h (114mph) of the old, and acceleration was better up to 100km/h, which took 12.3 seconds in a four-speed manual 190E 1.8 but 12.8 seconds in a carburettor 190.

That said, the 190E 1.8 was no ball of fire. The old 190 was already long past its sell-by date and was very pedestrian in comparison with most rival 2.0-litre saloons then on the market. So the 1.8-litre car more or less picked up where the old model had left off. It was quick enough for those who wanted the prestige and quality of a Mercedes saloon more than they wanted strong performance, but competitive it was not. Both five-speed and automatic gearboxes were available as alternatives to the standard four-speed manual, but the automatic was a particularly weak performer, taking 13 seconds to reach 100km/h from rest and peaking at 180km/h (112mph).

A pilot batch of the new 190E 1.8 model was assembled in January 1990 and the cars began to reach showrooms in March that year. Nevertheless, the old carburettor 190 was not replaced for all markets; it would in fact remain in production until January 1991. Mercedes' intention was to keep the 1.8-litre car as the entry-level model of the W201 range, keeping its cost down by minimizing standard equipment levels. Although these varied from one market to the next, probably a high proportion of the 190E 1.8 models built over the next three years or so had a fairly basic specification.

It was interesting that Mercedes had not anticipated the confusion that would arise over the naming of their new model. The designation 190E 1.8 in itself made perfect sense, as did others such as 190E 2.3. The problem that arose, however, was over the name of the original 190E. Customers seemed to have some difficulty in working out that this had a 2.0-litre engine. As a result, after a year it was renamed as 190E 2.0 and the confusion disappeared.

Press Reaction to the 190E 1.8

In Britain, *Autocar* magazine was able to try an early right-hand-drive automatic example and published its findings in the issue dated 5 December 1990. Mercedes-Benz UK had specified the car to make it an attractive alternative to a Ford Sierra Ghia, which admittedly came with more equipment than the Mercedes but also cost £20 more. To get to that price, however, the Mercedes had been stripped to the bone: 'Central locking excepted, just about everything that might be considered essential in any self-respecting mid-sized saloon carries a hefty, Mercedes option premium.'

Performance was not the car's best feature, and *Autocar* concluded that 'anyone seriously considering a 190E 1.8 with electric windows and sunroof (both standard on the 190E 2.0, together with improved trim materials) might well be tempted to spend a few hundred pounds extra for the performance benefits of the 2.0litre'. Although the 1.8-litre car 'feels spritely enough around town.... for overtaking out of city limits [it] requires space and time to build up momentum. Response is just too lethargic, even with kickdown.'

Car magazine for April 1991 had similar views, remarking on the car's 'indifferent, almost lacklustre powertrain'. With the automatic gearbox, 'overtaking bursts tend to be noisy, frenzied manoeuvres, not in keeping with the car's imperious stature'. Yet the comfort, handling and build quality were all deemed to be well up to Mercedes standards.

INTERIOR COLOURS FOR W201 MODELS, 1989–1991

Upholstery was available in Cloth, MB-Tex, Velours or Leather. Eight colours were available: Black, Blue, Brazil, Date, Cream Beige, Grey, Mid Red and Pine Green. Note that Velours never came in Black, but in Anthracite.

ONE THAT GOT AWAY: THE 201 CABRIOLET

Cabriolet conversions of the W201 range were available from aftermarket specialists at quite an early stage in the model's life (see Chapter 8). None of these had factory 'approval'; most were sold overseas, especially in the Middle East; and they were formidably expensive.

BMW had offered a convertible 3 Series as a regular production option since 1986, which must have rankled at Stuttgart. There was no doubt that the lines of the W201 would also work very well as a cabriolet, and Mercedes engineers were looking at the development of just such a car at about the time when they were working on a cabriolet version of the 124-series range. They based the single prototype on a 190E 2.6 model, which remained a secret at Stuttgart until Mercedes celebrated the 30th anniversary of its compact saloon range in 2012. At that stage, it was shown to selected members of the press as an interesting might-have-been.

Finished to a very high standard, with leather upholstery, the cabriolet prototype was very attractive. Although registered with a Stuttgart number since it became part of the Mercedes-Benz Historic Collection, it apparently spent some time wearing a number plate from Neu Ulm. Perhaps the point of this was to allow it to be tested on public roads without it being too obvious that it was actually a Mercedes prototype. Onlookers who realized that it was out of the ordinary might well have assumed that it was a conversion by one of the aftermarket specialists.

The execution of the 190 cabriolet prototype was not quite perfect. A close look would reveal that the plastic flank panels had actually been made by cutting-and-shutting saloon types, and the boot lid tended to foul the cover for the stowed cabriolet roof. The rear seat was also rather narrow and more work might have been needed to improve that. However, these were not major flaws; most development prototypes suffer from problems that are sorted out before the model they preview is brought to production.

The 124 cabriolet was successfully brought to market (initially as a 300CE-24) in September 1991, but the W201 cabriolet never became a production model. There were probably several reasons for this. One of them must have been the cost of developing a suitable two-door version of the four-door W201 saloon body. By contrast, the existence of the two-door coupé version of the 124 series made creating a two-door cabriolet much more straightforward.

The rising beltline that had always been a W201 characteristic gave the factory's own cabriolet prototype a most attractive appearance. It was based on a six-cylinder model.

The proposed W201 cabriolet also came too late to be viable as a production model. By 1990, when the prototype was built, the W201 range had just three years of production left. After subtracting a year from that to perfect the car and get it into production, it would have had a production life of only two years. It is unlikely that it would have sold enough to justify the cost of being put into production.

Paint Colours for W201 models, 1989–1991

German name	English name	Code	Model-year		
			1989	1990	1991
Beige					
Hellelfenbein	Taxi Beige/Light Ivory	623	✓	✓	✓
Pueblobeige	Pueblo Beige	651	✓	✓	✓
Black					
Schwarz	Black	040	✓	✓	✓
Blue					
Beryll	Beryll metallic	888		✓	✓
Diamantblau	Diamond Blue	355	✓		
Dunkelblau	Midnight Blue	904	✓	✓	✓
Nautikblau	Nautical Blue metallic	929	✓	✓	✓
Perlblau	Pearl Blue metallic	348		✓	✓
Petrol	Blue-Green metallic	877	✓		
Surfblau	Surf Blue	900	✓	✓	
Brown					
Bisonbraun	Havana Brown	432	✓		
Impala	Impala Brown	441	✓	✓	✓
Green					
Achatgrün	Agate Green	815	✓	✓	
Malachit	Malachite Green metallic	249		✓	✓
Nachtgrün	Pine Green metallic	254	✓		
Nelkengrün	Willow Green metallic	261	✓	✓	
Grey					
Anthrazitgrau	Anthracite Grey	172	✓	✓	✓
Blauschwarz	Blue-Black metallic	199	✓	✓	✓
Bornit	Bornite metallic	481		✓	✓
Carraragrau	Marble Grey	752		✓	✓
Liasgrau	Ascot Grey	751	✓		
Perlmuttgrau	Pearl Grey metallic	122	✓	✓	✓
Red					
Almandinrot	Almandine Red metallic	512	✓	✓	✓
Barolorot	Barolo Red	540	✓	✓	✓
Pajettrot	Pajett Red metallic	587	✓	✓	✓
Signalrot	Signal Red	568	✓	✓	✓
Silver					
Astralsilber	Astral Silver	735	✓		
Brillantsilber	Brilliant Silver	744		✓	✓
Rauchsilber	Smoke Silver	702	✓	✓	✓
White					
Arcticweiss	Arctic White	147	✓	✓	✓

Note: Rauchsilber was available only on the 190E 2.5-16.

TECHNICAL SPECIFICATIONS: MERCEDES-BENZ W201 MODELS, 1989–1991 MODEL-YEARS

Engine (190)
M102 four-cylinder with cast-iron block and alloy cylinder head
1997cc (89mm bore × 80.25mm stroke)
Single overhead camshaft, two valves per cylinder
Five-bearing crankshaft

ECE version
Compression ratio 9.1:1
Stromberg 175 CDT carburettor
Max. power 105PS at 5,200rpm
Max. torque 170Nm at 2,500rpm

RÜF version
Compression ratio 9.1:1
Pierburg 2E-E carburettor with electronic control
Max. power 105PS at 5,500rpm
Max. torque 165Nm at 3,000rpm

KAT version
Compression ratio 9.1:1
Pierburg 2E-E carburettor with electronic control
Max. power 102PS at 5,500rpm
Max. torque 160Nm at 3,000rpm

Engine (190E)
M102 four-cylinder with cast-iron block and alloy cylinder head
1997cc (89mm bore × 80.25mm stroke)
Single overhead camshaft, two valves per cylinder
Five-bearing crankshaft

RÜF version
Compression ratio 9.1:1
Bosch KE-Jetronic mechanical fuel injection
Max. power 122PS at 5,100rpm
Max. torque 178Nm at 3,500rpm

KAT version
Compression ratio 9.1:1
Bosch KE-Jetronic mechanical fuel injection
Max. power 118PS at 5,100rpm
Max. torque 172Nm at 3,500rpm

Engine (190E 1.8)
M102 four-cylinder with cast-iron block and alloy cylinder head
1797cc (89.0mm bore × 72.2mm stroke)
Single overhead camshaft, two valves per cylinder
Five-bearing crankshaft
Compression ratio 9.0:1
Bosch KE-Jetronic mechanical fuel injection
Max. power 109PS at 5,500rpm
Max. torque 150Nm at 3,700rpm

Engine (190E 2.3)
M102 four-cylinder with cast-iron block and alloy cylinder head
2299cc (95.5mm bore × 80.25mm stroke)
Single overhead camshaft, two valves per cylinder
Five-bearing crankshaft

RÜF version
Compression ratio 9.0:1
Bosch KE-Jetronic mechanical fuel injection
Max. power 136PS at 5,100rpm
Max. torque 205Nm at 3,500rpm

KAT version
Compression ratio 9.0:1
Bosch KE-Jetronic mechanical fuel injection
Max. power 132PS at 5,100rpm
Max. torque 198Nm at 3,500rpm

Engine (190E 2.5-16)
M102 four-cylinder with cast-iron block and alloy cylinder head
2498cc (95.5mm bore × 87.2mm stroke)
Two overhead camshafts, four valves per cylinder
Five-bearing crankshaft

RÜF version
Compression ratio 9.7:1
Bosch KE-Jetronic mechanical fuel injection
Max. power 204PS at 6,750rpm
Max. torque 240Nm at 5,500rpm

KAT version
Compression ratio 9.7:1
Bosch KE-Jetronic mechanical fuel injection
Max. power 195PS at 6,750rpm
Max. torque 235Nm at 5,000rpm

Engine (190E 2.5-16 Evolution I)
M102 four-cylinder with cast-iron block and alloy cylinder
head
2463cc (97.3mm bore × 82.8mm stroke)
Two overhead camshafts, four valves per cylinder
Five-bearing crankshaft

RÜF version
Compression ratio 9.7:1
Bosch KE-Jetronic mechanical fuel injection
Max. power 204PS at 6,750rpm
Max. torque 240Nm at 5,500rpm

KAT version
Compression ratio 9.7:1
Bosch KE-Jetronic mechanical fuel injection
Max. power 195PS at 6,750rpm
Max. torque 235Nm at 5,000rpm

Engine (190E 2.5-16 Evolution II)
M102 four-cylinder with cast-iron block and alloy cylinder
head
2463cc (97.3mm bore × 82.8mm stroke)
Two overhead camshafts, four valves per cylinder
Five-bearing crankshaft
Compression ratio 10.5:1
Bosch KE-Jetronic mechanical fuel injection
Max. power 235PS at 7,200rpm
Max. torque 245Nm from 5,000 to 6,000rpm

Engine (190E 2.6)
M103 six-cylinder with cast-iron block and alloy cylinder
head
2599cc (82.9mm bore × 80.25mm stroke)
Single overhead camshaft, two valves per cylinder
Four-bearing crankshaft

RÜF version
Compression ratio 9.2:1
Bosch KE-Jetronic mechanical fuel injection
Max. power 166PS at 5,800rpm
Max. torque 228Nm at 4,600rpm

KAT version
Compression ratio 9.2:1
Bosch KE-Jetronic mechanical fuel injection
Max. power 160PS at 5,800rpm
Max. torque 220Nm at 4,600rpm

Engine (190D)
OM601 four-cylinder diesel with cast-iron block and alloy
cylinder head
1997cc (87mm bore × 84mm stroke)
Single overhead camshaft, two valves per cylinder
Five-bearing crankshaft
Compression ratio 22:1
Indirect injection with Bosch pump
Max. power 72PS at 4,600rpm
  (75PS from March 1989)
Max. torque 123Nm at 2,800rpm
  (126Nm from 2,700 to 3,550rpm, from March 1989)

Engine (190D 2.5)
OM602 five-cylinder with cast-iron block and alloy cylinder
head
2497cc (87mm bore × 84mm stroke)
Single overhead camshaft, two valves per cylinder
Six-bearing crankshaft
Compression ratio 22:1
Indirect injection with Bosch pump
Max. power 90PS at 4,600rpm (94PS from March 1989)
Max. torque 154Nm at 2,800rpm (158Nm from 2,600 to
  3,100rpm, from March 1989)

Engine (190D 2.5 Turbo)
OM602 five-cylinder with cast-iron block and alloy cylinder
head
2497cc (87mm bore × 84mm stroke)
Single overhead camshaft, two valves per cylinder
Six-bearing crankshaft
Compression ratio 22:1
Indirect injection with Bosch pump and turbocharger
Max. power 126PS at 4,600rpm
Max. torque 231Nm at 2,400rpm

Gearbox
Four-speed manual GL68/20 D (190D)
  Ratios 4.23:1, 2.36:1, 1.49:1, 1.00:1, reverse 4.10:1
Four-speed manual GL68/20 H (190, 190E, 190E 1.8)
  Ratios 3.91:1, 2.17:1, 1.37:1, 1.00:1, reverse 3.78:1
Five-speed manual GL68/20 B-5 (190 to August 1989, 190E
to August 1989, 190D 2.5 to August 1989)
  Ratios 3.91:1, 2.17:1, 1.37:1, 1.00:1, 0.78:1, reverse 4.27:1
Five-speed manual GL68/20 C-5 (190D to August 1989, 190E
2.3 to August 1989)
  Ratios 3.91:1, 2.17:1, 1.37:1, 1.00:1, 0.78:1, reverse 4.27:1

Five-speed manual GL68/20 C-5 (190 from September 1989, 190E from September 1989, 190D 2.5 from September 1989, 190E 1.8)
Ratios 3.91:1, 2.17:1, 1.37:1, 1.00:1, 0.81:1, reverse 4.27:1
Five-speed manual GL68/20 D-5 (190D 2.5 from September 1989, 190E 2.3 from September 1989)
Ratios 3.91:1, 2.17:1, 1.37:1, 1.00:1, 0.81:1, reverse 4.27:1
Five-speed manual GL76/27 C-5 (190E 2.6)
Ratios 3.86:1, 2.18:1, 1.38:1, 1.00:1, 0.80:1, reverse 4.22:1
Five-speed close-ratio manual GL275 E (190E 2.5-16, Evo I, Evo II)
Ratios 4.08:1, 2.52:1, 1.77:1, 1.26:1, 1.00:1, reverse 4.16:1
Five-speed manual GL76/27 F-5 (190D from September 1989)
Ratios 3.91:1, 2.17:1, 1.37:1, 1.00:1, 0.81:1, reverse 4.27:1
Four-speed automatic W4A 020 (190, 190E, 190E 2.3, 190E 2.5-16, 190E 2.6, 190D, 190D 2.5, 190D 2.5 Turbo, 190E 1.8)
Ratios 4.25:1, 2.41:1, 1.49:1, 1.00:1, reverse 5.67:1
Torque converter multiplication 2.2

The GL68/20 C-5 and GL68/20 D-5 gearboxes were alternatives for the 190D 2.5 from September 1989.

Axle ratio
2.65:1 (190D 2.5 Turbo)
3.07:1 (190E 2.5-16, 190E 2.6 automatic, 190D 2.5 automatic)
3.23:1 (190E, 190D)
3.27:1 (190E 2.3 to August 1989, 190E 2.3 automatic, 190E 2.5-16 Evo I, 190E 2.6 five-speed to August 1989)
3.46:1 (190, 190E five-speed, 190E 2.3 from September 1989, 190E 2.5-16 Evo II, 190E 1.8)
3.64:1 (190D 2.5 five-speed, 190E 1.8 five-speed)
3.91:1 (190D five-speed)
3.92:1 (190E 2.6 five-speed from September 1989)

Suspension
Front suspension with MacPherson struts, wishbones, coil springs, telescopic gas dampers and anti-roll bar; height adjustment optional on 190E 2.5-16; hydro-pneumatic height adjustment on Evo I and Evo II.
Rear suspension with five links, coil springs, telescopic gas dampers and anti-roll bar; hydro-pneumatic self-levelling strut standard on 190E 2.5-16, Evo I, Evo II and optional on other models.

Steering
Recirculating-ball steering with power assistance.

Brakes
Disc brakes on all four wheels, ventilated at the front on 190E 2.5-16, Evo I, Evo II and 190E 2.6; dual hydraulic circuit and servo assistance; ABS optional (standard on 190E 2.5-16, Evo I, Evo II and 190E 2.6).

Dimensions
Overall length: 4,448mm (4,430mm for 190E 2.5-16, Evo I and Evo II)
Overall width: 1,690 mm
1,706mm for 190E 2.5-16
1,720mm for Evo I
Overall height: 1,375mm
1,353mm for Sportline option
1,361mm for 190E 2.5-16
1,342mm for Evo I and Evo II (standard settings); minimum 1,327mm and maximum 1,372mm
Wheelbase: 2,665mm
Track, front: 1,441mm
1,446mm for 190E 2.5-16
1,452mm for Sportline option
1,478mm for Evo I and Evo II
Track, rear: 1,421mm
1,431mm for 190E 2.5-16
1,432mm for Sportline option
1,453mm for Evo I and Evo II

Wheels and tyres
6J × 15 steel disc wheels with 185/65 R 15 tyres
6J × 15 alloy wheels with 185/65 R 15 tyres optional
7J × 15 alloy wheels with 205/55 VR 15 tyres, for 190E 2.5-16 and Sportline option
8J × 16 alloy wheels with 225/50 ZR 16 tyres, for Evo I
8.25J × 17 alloy wheels with 245/40 ZR 17 tyres, for Evo II

Running weight
190: 1,160kg
190E: 1,170kg
190E 1.8: 1,160kg
190E 2.3: 1,220kg
190E 2.5-16: 1,300kg
Evolution I: 1,320kg
Evolution II: 1,320kg
190E 2.6: 1,220kg
190D: 1,180kg
190D 2.5: 1,230kg
190D 2.5 Turbo: 1,300kg

THE FINAL YEARS

The final period of the W201's production life may be said to have begun in January 1991 – the date when several minor changes were made. There was one major change, in that the carburettor 190 finally went out of production. That then left eight models still available outside North America. Those with diesel engines were the 190D, 190D 2.5 and 190D 2.5 Turbo. The petrol models were the 190E 1.8, the 190E 2.0, the 190E 2.3, the 190E 2.5-16 and the 190E 2.6.

The 190E 2.0 deserves special but brief comment. As the previous chapter explains, there had been some customer confusion after the introduction of the 190E 1.8 just under a year earlier. As a result, Mercedes decided to rename the original 2.0-litre 190E as a 190E 2.0 and to give it the appro-

priate boot-lid badges. The opportunity was also taken to put power back up to the 122PS that the car had enjoyed before it was fitted with a catalytic converter. The power gain, of 4PS, was achieved by fitting a less restrictive twin-pipe exhaust system.

This was also the point at which Mercedes made ABS standard on all models, except for the entry-level 190D and 190E 1.8 types. At the same time, the dashboard was modified with a downwards central extension that united it with the centre console, and body-colour mirrors were made standard on all models except the 190D and 190E 1.8. The fixed mirror bases nevertheless remained in unpainted black plastic; only the adjustable head sections were painted.

The 1992 models were distinguished by body-colour door mirrors, as on this UK-market car. UK cars had come as standard with side repeater indicators, as seen here, for several years. NEWSPRESS/ AUTOCAR MAGAZINE

THE AUSTRALIAN 180E, 1991

There was one little-known but interesting variant of the W201 range that was created specifically for the Australian market and was sold only in that country. Introduced in October 1991 as a 1992 model, it was based on the 190E 1.8 and went by the name of the 180E Limited Edition. The boot lid carried a simple 180E badge on the left-hand side.

Just how limited was that limited edition, though? It is true that Mercedes in Aus-

Once again, the 190E 1.8 was not easy to distinguish from its siblings unless the badges on the boot lid were visible.

tralia were feeling the pressure from BMW's cheaper entry-level 318i model and from the Audi 80, with its aerodynamic looks and zinc-coated bodyshell. To alleviate this, the company set about creating a Mercedes that was very competitively priced, to avoid the luxury tax that was then levied on cars that cost more than around A$45,500. The 190E 1.8, which was already the cheapest and least well-equipped Mercedes model, was an obvious starting point. In order to reduce its price even further, Mercedes Australia successfully managed a deal that saw import duties offset against credits it had gained by using Australian-made components for its whole range. These components included springs and windscreen glass, as well as some other parts. The result was that the company was able to slash the showroom price quite dramatically. When it was initially released, a 180E Limited Edition cost just A$45,450, as compared with the A$63,200 required for a 190E 2.0.

The 180E Limited Edition did retain a few luxury features that Australians considered essential – the cars came with an automatic gearbox as standard (although a five-speed manual was optional) and with power steering, central locking and air conditioning. However, there was no ABS on the early cars (and it was not standard in Europe, either), the windows had manual winders and the seats were manually adjusted; there was neither cruise control nor heated door mirrors, and there was no multi-speaker ICE system either.

The sales brochure for the new 1.8-litre model demonstrated a more interesting approach than those for earlier models.

Unlike the 2.0-litre model, the car also lacked a centre front armrest and rear head restraints.

Despite its shortcomings, the 180E Limited Edition was a big hit in Australia, where it provided the prestige and build quality of a Mercedes-Benz without the expense. Mercedes Australia continued to sell examples right up until March 1994, when the new W202 C Class models replaced the last of the W201s.

Unique to Australia was a model badged as the 180E. The chrome wheel-arch highlights on this example were not part of the original specification. OSX/WIKIMEDIA COMMONS, PUBLIC DOMAIN

The 180E badge was cast specially and of course used the same font as the standard 190 type.

SPECIAL EDITIONS

1992 and 1993

In 1992 and 1993, Mercedes produced several special-edition models that were intended to give a fillip to sales, as some customers hesitated over whether to buy now or to wait for the new W202 C Class model that would replace the W201 just over a year later. There were some for Europe in 1992, some for the UK and Eire in 1993, and some for the USA in 1993 as well (for more on the latter, see Chapter 6).

For Europe, three special run-out editions were introduced in March 1992. Mercedes used them to explore design ideas. The colour schemes and interior appointments were the work of an international team of MB designers,

UK SPECIFICATIONS

As far as possible, Mercedes always built its W201 to a common specification, although the special requirements of the US market (see Chapter 6) did complicate things on the assembly lines to some extent. There were other variations from one country to another, where the local branch of the company was responsible for proposing a specification that was most suited to local conditions.

All this meant that specifications outside Germany were sometimes out of step with those for Mercedes' home market. Specifications varied from year to year, as importers tried to keep the cars competitive with rival models; sometimes, items would be deleted or reinstated in order to keep the basic models to a particular price.

As an illustration of this, it is interesting to see the changes that were made for the UK market in the last few years of W201 production. At this stage, the UK only took a selection from the eight models produced in Germany. The petrol models were the 190E 1.8, the 190E (2.0), the 190E 2.5-16 and the 190E 2.6. Up to the point of the car's discontinuation, at the end of 1990, UK customers could also buy a carburettor 190. The diesels were the 190D and 190D 2.5, but the UK was still a poor market for diesel passenger cars.

For clarity, the changes are shown in chronological order as a timeline.

September 1990: Catalytic converters standard on all petrol models; 190 (carburettor) discontinued
May 1991: Electric windows and sunroof now a cost option for 190E 2.0
August 1991: Luxury option package for 190E 2.0, consisting of automatic gearbox, electric windows and sunroof
October 1992: ABS and driver's airbag standard on all models; manual sunroof for 190E 2.0
January 1993: 190E 2.5-16 discontinued
April 1993: 190LE special editions introduced
September 1993: W201 imports ended; W202 C Class imports began in October

who used fresh and modern colours to give the range, now nearly ten years old, a younger and more modern appeal. To some extent, they were also used to prepare buyers for the brighter interiors that would be a feature of the new W202 C Class.

With these special editions, Mercedes hoped to draw younger buyers into the showrooms. The promotional literature suggested that the idea was to break the mould and to show that there could be more to a Mercedes than many people thought. However, those younger buyers had to be wealthy ones, because the special edition cars were vastly more expensive than their standard equivalents.

The cars were rolled out with the collective name of 'Avantgarde' (although the name was not used in the same way as it was later, when it became the Mercedes designator for sporty equipment alongside 'Classic', or basic, and 'Elegance', or luxury). The special editions were based on three strong-selling models of the range, and each one was quite distinctive. The Avantgarde Rosso was based on a 190E 1.8 with five-speed gearbox, the Avantgarde Azzurro was based on a 190E 2.3 and the Avantgarde Verde was based on a 190D 2.5. All were made exclusively with left-hand drive and were sold only on the European continent.

Starting at the bottom, the Avantgarde Rosso was both the cheapest and the most numerous of these special cars. Its price in Germany was DM49,875 (when a standard 190E 1.8 cost DM35,910), and a total of 2,300 were built. Described by the sales brochure as the 'arty model', it was painted in a pearlescent metallic red that was set off by 15-hole alloy wheels. Inside the passenger cabin, the seats were upholstered in a material called Arcade, which Mercedes claimed had been inspired by modern art museums and by New York graffiti art.

The mid-range car was the Avantgarde Verde, supposedly aimed at the ecologically minded customer. This was finished in a micatallic dark green paint, complemented by Anton interior fabric that combined black-on-green and green-on-black themes. This one was priced at DM54,500, when a standard 190D 2.5 cost DM44,118 without extras; just 750 were built.

In Europe, the least expensive of the run-out limited editions was the Rosso, based on a 190E 1.8.

The Rosso Red colour used for the limited edition was not made available on regular production models, but it did suit the car very well.

The upholstery in the Rosso model was extremely eye-catching. It did not (perhaps fortunately) presage a new approach at Mercedes.

By far the most expensive of these special editions was the Avantgarde Azzurro, of which 950 were built. Each car cost DM 65,500, when a standard 190E 2.3 without extras was priced at DM 45,885. This one had the Sportline package, with lowered suspension, wider alloy wheels and tyres, sharper steering and sports seats. The upholstery was essentially black leather, but each seat had a different coloured highlight and there were door trims and carpets to match. In this case, the paintwork was an attractive micatallic blue.

Country-Specific Limited Editions

In addition to the expensive Avantgarde models, Mercedes built other limited-edition models for specific countries as W201 production approached its end. For Switzerland, for example, a special Primavera Edition was announced at the Geneva motor show in March 1992. This was essentially a variant of the Avantgarde Verde model that came with the eight-hole alloy wheels that were available on some other Mercedes models. The eight-hole alloy wheels also appeared on a Black Edition that was sold in Italy.

In Germany, there were two very interesting editions. The Berlin 2000 Edition was released in August 1992 to highlight Berlin's bid to host the 2000 Summer Olympic Games. (In fact, Berlin was unsuccessful and Sydney was chosen as the host city.) There were 190 Berlin 2000 cars, all car-

The striking colour and the high equipment levels lifted the Rosso edition far above the regular 1.8-litre car, but of course the badge on the boot lid revealed that it was based on the entry-level W201.

As the boot-lid numbers make clear, the Azzurro limited edition was based on the mid-range 2.3-litre car. It was once again exceptionally attractive. Mercedes doubtless wanted to see what sort of reception such bright colours would get from customers.

There was another multi-coloured interior for the Azzurro limited edition, but once again it did not lead to anything longer-lasting in the Mercedes range.

There was a rather different approach to the interior of the Verde, with its interesting combination of green and black; even the wood trim had a green finish. The Avantgarde identification plaque is clearly visible here on the glovebox lid.

rying special decals and all with the Sportline options and AMG alloy wheels. They were based on the 190E 1.8, the 190E 2.3 and the 190E 3.2 AMG (see Chapter 8), and all were painted in Brilliant Silver. The second edition was the DTM '92, which marked the success of the works racers in the 1992 DTM. It came as a 190E 1.8 or a 190E 2.3, in each case with the Sportline options and in a choice of Brilliant Silver or Blue-Black metallic.

Finished in a third attractive colour, the Verde edition was based on the five-cylinder diesel model. Mercedes clearly believed the time was right to explore brighter paints, perhaps in order to give the W202 C Class models that followed the W201s a more modern image.

The 190LE, 1993

Although right-hand-drive markets were denied the special Avantgarde editions in autumn 1992, Britain and Eire were not left out completely. From April 1993, the two countries were given a pair of special-edition models that were more specifically tailored to their needs and tastes. Based on the 190E 1.8 and the 190E 2.0, these were generically known as the 190LE (or 'Limited Edition'). Each example carried a neat metal LE badge in standard Mercedes-style lettering on the right-hand side of the boot lid.

Quite unlike the Avantgarde editions sold in Europe, the 190LE cars were run-out editions that were intended to offer customers a special value-for-money package. They were also designed to attract customers into the showroom in the hope that, even if they did not buy one of the special-edition cars, they might be persuaded to buy a standard model.

At the time, a standard 190E 1.8 saloon cost £17,300 in Britain; with all the extras that were part of the LE package, its price would have been £22,767.54. The LE, however, cost £19,245. Similarly, a standard 190E 2.0 cost £19,245, or £23,878.78 with all the extras that came as standard on the LE, while the LE itself cost just £21,630. Although no definitive figures for the individual types have yet been discovered, it is generally accepted that there were 1,000 examples of the 190LE in total. Each one came with a large (A3) printed certificate that carried its unique number within the special edition.

The 190LE models came in three colours, of which two were shared with the earlier European special editions.

These were the attractive metallic Azzurro Blue and the similarly striking micatallic Rosso Red. The third colour was the 'safe' option, Brilliant Silver, drawn from the standard colour palette. Each colour came with one specific interior treatment. The Azzurro cars had grey check cloth upholstery; the Rosso cars had a checked cloth in beige and cream; and the Brilliant Silver cars had black checked cloth upholstery.

Both the 1.8-litre and 2.0-litre types came with an automatic gearbox, with ABS and with the eight-hole alloy wheels not otherwise available on the W201 models. All cars had electric windows, an electric sunroof, a driver's airbag, a front centre armrest, rear head restraints and a Blaupunkt Verona CR43 stereo radio-cassette player. A windscreen top shade band was a further special item. They also had another feature not seen elsewhere on the W201 range:

MERCEDES' SUPPLEMENTARY RESTRAINT SYSTEM

For the W201's final year in production, Mercedes increased equipment levels, using a strategy that was commonly used to discourage buyers from delaying a purchase until a new model appeared. From October 1992, central locking and an airbag were standardized across the range, and ABS was finally made standard on the entry-level 190D and 190E 1.8 models.

Airbags were not of course new to the W201 range. A driver's airbag was part of the Mercedes SRS (Supplementary Restraint System), which had been optional at extra cost since the model's introduction, and had been standard on all W201s sold in the USA. The system consisted of an airbag mounted within the hub of the steering wheel, plus a seat-belt pre-tensioning system.

The airbag was activated by a sensor mounted at the front of the transmission tunnel. This sensor responded to forward deceleration approximately equivalent to a 12mph collision with a rigid barrier, triggering a detonator that ignited a charge of sodium azide, a colourless but toxic salt. A rapid chemical reaction followed and produced a large volume of nearly pure nitrogen gas that inflated the neoprene-coated nylon airbag in 0.03 seconds. As the bag inflated, it would push a hinged plastic cover clear of the driver's impact zone.

As the driver hit the inflated airbag, the nitrogen gas would be forced out of it through slots around its sides. The impact with the bag would help to decelerate the driver's forward movement, and the airbag would typically be fully deflated within 0.10 seconds after inflation.

The Mercedes SRS system used the same motion sensor to trigger a small powder charge that turned the reels of the two front seat belts to take up any slack. The theory behind this was that the tightened belts would reduce the severity of injuries in a collision.

Some countries had their own special editions. This black one for Italy came with the attractive eight-spoke alloy wheels introduced in June 1993 on the last 124-series cars. STAHLKOCHER/WIKIMEDIA COMMONS

THE MERCEDES-BENZ 190LE

a Limited Edition available for a limited period only

Sales brochure for the 190 LE, which was sold in the UK and in Eire. Limited editions were used to boost sales late in the production run of the W201.

polished Burr Walnut wood trim in place of the standard Zebrano wood. The sales brochure pointed out that no other options could be added on the assembly lines — these cars were obviously built as a batch — but dealers were able to add some extra features at the point of sale if the customer asked for them.

THE END OF THE LINE

By the end of 1992, the W201 range had been on sale for ten years. Mercedes had been working on its W202 C Class successor since the middle of the 1980s. Pilot production of some early variants had begun as early as August 1992, with volume production beginning in the first few months of 1993.

Nevertheless, there would be a considerable overlap in production between the old and new compact Mercedes, with W201 production being closed down gradually. Assembly at the Sindelfingen plant stopped first, in February 1993, but production at Bremen (mainly for export) continued for several more months. The first model to be taken out of production was the 190E 2.5-16, of which the last example was built in June. On hand for a brief celebratory ceremony was Klaus Ludwig, who had driven a racing version to victory in the DTM series a few months earlier.

The rest continued until August, when the German production lines shut down for good and the last car of all was handed over to the Mercedes-Benz Museum. Various overall production totals have been quoted over the years, but the one that Mercedes themselves now quote is 1,879,630. For a model-by-model breakdown of this figure, *see* Appendix III.

The final 190 E 2.5-16 left the production line in Bremen on 17 May 1993. Klaus Ludwig, who won the 1992 DTM Championship in a related Evolution II model, was on hand to give it a proper send-off.

THE 190 ELEKTRO

Mercedes-Benz had a long history of experimenting with alternatives to the internal combustion engine. One of the options it examined with some determination was electric power. In April 1982, around eight months before the introduction of the W201 range, the company displayed an experimental electric model based on a 123-series estate car at the Hanover Trade Fair.

The main power unit was a 30kW (41PS) electric motor, which was fed by a large quantity of nickel-iron batteries (the most advanced type at the time), stored in a huge tray that took up all the floor space in the load area. These batteries were enormously heavy, with a weight of 600kg, and the vehicle had a top speed of only about 50mph (80km/h); it also had a two-cylinder petrol engine that added an 'emergency' range of 30 miles (48km) in case the batteries became exhausted. It was a brave attempt, but at this stage it was very clear that the concept of battery power was still very far from viable for a production car.

For much of the rest of the 1980s, Mercedes focused on experiments with hydrogen-powered engines, but by the end of the decade the company was ready once again to look at battery power. This time, it chose a W201 saloon as the host vehicle, and at the Geneva show in March 1991 it presented the 190E Elektro.

The Elektro was still very much an experimental vehicle. Power came from a pair of permanent-magnet DC electric motors mounted under the bonnet, each one delivering 19kW (26PS). Unusually for an electric vehicle, they drove through a five-speed manual gearbox. The batteries were the latest sodium-nickel-chloride types, housed under the bonnet. A plug allowed them to be recharged from an electric charging point. Battery condition and other gauges were incorporated on the dashboard in a multi-instrument dial that replaced the standard clock.

The normal range for the car between charges was about 80km (50 miles), although that increased to a theoretical 175km (109 miles) at a constant 50km/h (31mph). There was a maximum speed of 114km/h (71mph), although the car was probably slow to

A 190 Elektro pictured on the island of Rügen in the Baltic during the four-year test programme there. Sadly, the experiment served largely to confirm that electric-powered cars were not yet viable for general use.

One 190 Elektro survives in Mercedes ownership, although it is no longer driveable. This particular car racked up 100,000km on test between 1992 and 1995. Interestingly, the number plate reads '190 E Elektro', although the cars were always known as plain 190 Elektro models when they were in use.

The underbonnet view of the surviving Elektro car. The larger box on the left houses a charging and control unit; the white box houses a battery control system.

reach such speeds; its total weight was 1,575kg (3,472lb), or about 405kg (893lb) more than a standard petrol 190E 2.0, thanks mainly to the storage batteries.

In 1992, Mercedes provided ten of these cars for a four-year electric vehicle experiment on the tourist island of Rügen in the Baltic Sea. The company also provided a similar number of other vehicles, which were joined by experimental prototypes from BMW, Opel and Volkswagen. Three of the W201s that Mercedes supplied for the test had the five-speed gearbox. The other seven had an asynchronous engine layout, with no separate transmission. Interestingly, it appears that the cars were converted from standard production types, and at least one of them carried the VIN of a 190D with that model's 201.122 prefix. (The full VIN was WDB2011221A694573.)

The primary aim was to test the vehicles

in advance of the Californian requirement that 2 per cent of all cars sold in the state should be zero-emission types by 1998. A group of fifty-eight inhabitants of this very flat island were given an electric car to use for the duration, and quickly discovered the disadvantages of electric power at that stage of its development. Hills presented problems, batteries often ran out of charge at critical moments, users complained of lack of performance, and there was a general feeling that all the cars were temperamental. Mercedes themselves admitted later that there were still some unresolved problems: the batteries could reach a temperature of 300° Celsius when in use, and the cars had not been crash-tested in their electric form. (To view a short video of the Mercedes trials, go to You Tube and search for #w201 #ElectricCar #Mercedes190.)

As preserved, the Elektro car now has a clear panel in the bonnet to allow its electrical system to be seen more easily. This was not fitted when the cars were on test in Rügen.

Needless to say, no volume production of 190 Elektro models was ever undertaken. Many years later, when Mercedes was celebrating thirty years of the W201, in 2012, the company showed one of the Elektro cars to selected journalists. The car had been driven for 100,000 test kilometres but was sadly no longer mobile, as its batteries had deteriorated and had been removed.

There were two types of Elektro 190. This view of the front-mounted battery pack (with its cover removed) shows several differences from the layout in the red car.

With the battery pack removed, the primary traction motor can be seen, linked to the front end of a standard five-speed gearbox.

Paint Colours for W201 models, 1992–1993

German name	English name	Code	Model-year	
			1992	**1993**
Beige				
Hellelfenbein	Taxi Beige/Light Ivory	623	✓	✓
Black				
Schwarz	Black	040	✓	✓
Blue				
Avantgardeblau	Avant Garde Blue micatallic	343	✓	
Beryll	Beryll metallic	888	✓	✓
Dunkelblau	Midnight Blue	904	✓	✓
Nautikblau	Nautical Blue metallic	929	✓	✓
Perlblau	Pearl Blue metallic	348	✓	✓
Brown				
Nutria	Nutria Brown	475	✓	✓
Rosenholz	Rosewood	485	✓	✓
Green				
Avantgardegrün	Avant Garde Green Micatallic	269	✓	
Kristallgrün	Crystal Green metallic	256	✓	✓
Malachit	Malachite Green metallic	249	✓	✓
Grey				
Anthrazitgrau	Anthracite Grey	172	✓	✓
Blauschwarz	Blue-Black metallic	199	✓	✓
Bornit	Bornite	481	✓	✓
Carraragrau	Marble Grey	752	✓	
Perlmuttgrau	Pearl Grey metallic	122	✓	✓
Red				
Almandinrot	Almandine Red metallic	512	✓	✓
Avantgarderot	Avant Garde Red micatallic	569	✓	
Barolorot	Barolo Red	540	✓	✓
Signalrot	Signal Red	568	✓	✓
Silver				
Brillantsilber	Brilliant Silver	744	✓	✓
Rauchsilber	Smoke Silver	702	✓	✓
White				
Arcticweiss	Arctic White	147	✓	✓

Note: Rauchsilber was available only on the 190E 2.5-16.

INTERIOR COLOURS FOR W201 MODELS, 1992–1993

Upholstery was available in Cloth, MB-Tex, Velours or Leather. Eight colours were available: Black, Blue, Brazil, Date, Cream Beige, Grey, Mid Red and Pine Green. Note that Velours never came in Black, but in Anthracite. There were three special finishes for the Avantgarde models in 1992: Multi-coloured cloth with Black bolsters (for the Rosso), Black with Green cloth (for the Verde) and Black leather with coloured highlights (for the Azzurro).

TECHNICAL SPECIFICATIONS: MERCEDES-BENZ W201 MODELS, 1991–1993 MODEL-YEARS

Engine (190E 1.8)

M102 four-cylinder with cast-iron block and alloy cylinder head

1797cc (89.0mm bore × 72.2mm stroke)

Single overhead camshaft, two valves per cylinder

Five-bearing crankshaft

Compression ratio 9.0:1

Bosch KE-Jetronic mechanical fuel injection

Max. power 109PS at 5,500rpm

Max. torque 150Nm at 3,700rpm

Engine (190E 2.0)

M102 four-cylinder with cast-iron block and alloy cylinder head

1997cc (89mm bore × 80.25mm stroke)

Single overhead camshaft, two valves per cylinder

Five-bearing crankshaft

Compression ratio 9.1:1

Bosch KE-Jetronic mechanical fuel injection

Max. power 122PS at 5,300rpm

Max. torque 175Nm at 3,500rpm

Engine (190E 2.3)

M102 four-cylinder with cast-iron block and alloy cylinder head

2299cc (95.5mm bore × 80.25mm stroke)

Single overhead camshaft, two valves per cylinder

Five-bearing crankshaft

Compression ratio 9.0:1

Bosch KE-Jetronic mechanical fuel injection

Max. power 136PS at 5,200rpm

Max. torque 200Nm at 3,500rpm

Engine (190E 2.5-16)

M102 four-cylinder with cast-iron block and alloy cylinder head

2498cc (95.5mm bore × 87.2mm stroke)

Two overhead camshafts, four valves per cylinder

Five-bearing crankshaft

Compression ratio 9.7:1

Bosch KE-Jetronic mechanical fuel injection

Max. power 195PS at 6,750rpm

Max. torque 235Nm from 5,000 to 5,500rpm

Engine (190E 2.6)

M103 six-cylinder with cast-iron block and alloy cylinder head

2599cc (82.9mm bore × 80.25mm stroke)

Single overhead camshaft, two valves per cylinder

Four-bearing crankshaft

Compression ratio 9.2:1

Bosch KE-Jetronic mechanical fuel injection

Max. power 160PS at 5,800rpm

Max. torque 220Nm at 4,600rpm

Engine (190D)

OM601 four-cylinder diesel with cast-iron block and alloy cylinder head

1997cc (87mm bore x 84mm stroke)

Single overhead camshaft, two valves per cylinder

Five-bearing crankshaft

Compression ratio 22:1

Indirect injection with Bosch pump

Max. power 75PS at 4,600rpm

Max. torque 126Nm at 2,800rpm

Engine (190D 2.5)

OM602 five-cylinder with cast-iron block and alloy cylinder head

2497cc (87mm bore × 84mm stroke)

Single overhead camshaft, two valves per cylinder

Six-bearing crankshaft

Compression ratio 22:1

Indirect injection with Bosch pump

Max. power 94PS at 4,600rpm

Max. torque 158Nm from 2,600 to 3,100rpm

Engine (190D 2.5 Turbo)

OM602 five-cylinder with cast-iron block and alloy cylinder head

2497cc (87mm bore × 84mm stroke)

Single overhead camshaft, two valves per cylinder

Six-bearing crankshaft

Compression ratio 22:1

Indirect injection with Bosch pump and turbocharger

126PS at 4,600rpm

231Nm at 2,400rpm

Gearbox

Four-speed manual GL68/20 D (190D)

 Ratios 4.23:1, 2.36:1, 1.49:1, 1.00:1, reverse 4.10:1

Four-speed manual GL68/20 H (190, 190E, 190E 1.8)

 Ratios 3.91:1, 2.17:1, 1.37:1, 1.00:1, reverse 3.78:1

Five-speed manual GL68/20 B-5 (190 to August 1989, 190E to August 1989, 190D 2.5 to August 1989)

 Ratios 3.91:1, 2.17:1, 1.37:1, 1.00:1, 0.78:1, reverse 4.27:1

Five-speed manual GL68/20 C-5 (190D to August 1989, 190E 2.3 to August 1989)

 Ratios 3.91:1, 2.17:1, 1.37:1, 1.00:1, 0.78:1, reverse 4.27:1

Five-speed manual GL68/20 C-5 (190 from September 1989, 190E from September 1989, 190D 2.5 from September 1989, 190E 1.8)

 Ratios 3.91:1, 2.17:1, 1.37:1, 1.00:1, 0.81:1, reverse 4.27:1

Five-speed manual GL68/20 D-5 (190D 2.5 from September 1989, 190E 2.3 from September 1989)

 Ratios 3.91:1, 2.17:1, 1.37:1, 1.00:1, 0.81:1, reverse 4.27:1

Five-speed manual GL76/27 C-5 (190E 2.6)

 Ratios 3.86:1, 2.18:1, 1.38:1, 1.00:1, 0.80:1, reverse 4.22:1

Five-speed close-ratio manual GL275 E (190E 2.5-16)

 Ratios 4.08:1, 2.52:1, 1.77:1, 1.26:1, 1.00:1, reverse 4.16:1

Five-speed manual GL76/27 F-5 (190D from September 1989)

 Ratios 3.91:1, 2.17:1, 1.37:1, 1.00:1, 0.81:1, reverse 4.27:1

Four-speed automatic W4A 020 (190, 190E, 190E 2.3, 190E 2.5-16, 190E 2.6, 190D, 190D 2.5, 190D 2.5 Turbo, 190E 1.8)

 Ratios 4.25:1, 2.41:1, 1.49:1, 1.00:1, reverse 5.67:1

Note: The GL68/20 C-5 and GL68/20 D-5 gearboxes were alternatives for the 190D 2.5.

Axle ratio

2.65:1 (190D 2.5 Turbo)

3.07:1 (190E 2.5-16, 190E 2.6 automatic, 190D 2.5 automatic)

3.23:1 (190E, 190D)

3.27:1 (190E 2.3 automatic)

3.46:1 (190, 190E five-speed, 190E 2.3, 190E 1.8)

3.64:1 (190D 2.5 five-speed, 190E 1.8 five-speed)

3.91:1 (190D five-speed)

3.92:1 (190E 2.6 five-speed)

Suspension

Front suspension with MacPherson struts, wishbones, coil springs, telescopic gas dampers and anti-roll bar; height adjustment optional on 190E 2.5-16.

Rear suspension with five links, coil springs, telescopic gas dampers and anti-roll bar; hydro-pneumatic self-levelling strut standard on 190E 2.5-16 and optional on other models.

Steering

Recirculating-ball steering with power assistance.

Brakes

Disc brakes on all four wheels, ventilated at the front on 190E 2.5-16, Evo I, Evo II and 190E 2.6; dual hydraulic circuit and servo assistance; ABS optional (standard on 190E 2.5-16, Evo I, Evo II and 190E 2.6).

Dimensions

Overall length: 4,448mm (4,430mm for 190E 2.5-16)

Overall width: 1,690 mm

 1,706mm for 190E 2.5-16

 1,720mm for Evo I

Overall height: 1,375mm

 1,353mm with Sportline option

 1,361mm for 190E 2.5-16

Wheelbase: 2,665mm

Track, front: 1,441mm

 1,446mm for 190E 2.5-16

 1,452mm for Sportline option

Track, rear: 1,421mm

 1,431mm for 190E 2.5-16

 1,432mm for Sportline option

Wheels and tyres

6J × 15 steel disc wheels with 185/65 R 15 tyres

6J × 15 alloy wheels with 185/65 R 15 tyres optional

7J × 15 alloy wheels with 205/55 VR 15 tyres, for 190E 2.5-16 and Sportline option

Running weight

190: 1,160kg

190E: 1,170kg

190E 1.8: 1,160kg

190E 2.3: 1,220kg

190E 2.5-16: 1,300kg

190E 2.6: 1,220kg

190D: 1,180kg

190D 2.5: 1,230kg

190D 2.5 Turbo: 1,300kg

CHAPTER SIX

BORN FOR THE USA

Sales in North America, and more particularly in the USA, had become an essential part of the Mercedes business plan by the 1970s. Since the middle of the 1950s, the company had carefully built up a strong following across the Atlantic, establishing a reputation for making extremely well-engineered and well-built models. The high cost of the cars had ensured that ownership of a Mercedes was a symbol of prestige and wealth. Indeed, it was the first marque mentioned in American singer Janis Joplin's ironic anti-consumerism song of 1970: 'Oh Lord, won't you buy me a Mercedes-Benz?'

Operating at the top end of the market, and building cars that were not renowned for their fuel economy, Mercedes was quick to sense the impending doom of the first Oil Crisis in 1973. The W201 range itself was ultimately a reaction to the threat that the fuel shortage posed to Mercedes sales globally, but the problem in the USA was unique. As was the case in other countries, the cost of fuel at the pumps rose alarmingly after a major increase in the price of crude oil. However, the US government tackled the problem in its own way, reasoning that the problem would be mitigated if manufacturers were required to reduce the fuel consumption of their new cars.

In 1975 the US Congress introduced a new set of regulations designed to tackle high fuel consumption. Known as the Corporate Average Fuel Economy regulations, or CAFE rules for short, in simple terms they enabled the US government to fine any car maker if the average fuel consumption of all the cars and light trucks it sold in a given year exceeded a set figure. In addition, there was to be a Gas Guzzler Tax on any passenger car model (but not on light trucks) that did not achieve a set consumption figure.

For a maker with a range that included both small economy cars and large luxury saloons, the balance was not hugely difficult to achieve. However, for a company such as Mercedes-Benz, which sold only relatively large cars with thirsty engines, the CAFE regulations had potentially serious consequences. Stuttgart normally operated with quite long

model cycles, giving plenty of time for the thorough development of new models, and it was simply not possible to get a new and more fuel-efficient passenger car ready for the USA within the time-frame allowed before the CAFE rules became effective.

Mercedes went for a radical solution. Diesel-engined cars were much more fuel-efficient than petrol-engined cars, and Mercedes already had four decades of expertise in building them. The superior fuel economy of diesel cars was already beginning to tempt US buyers and there was a good chance that the market would witness a boom in diesel sales. The company therefore decided to offset the high fuel consumption of its larger and more prestigious models by selling large quantities of (relatively) frugal diesel types. At this point, no diesel Mercedes had ever been sold in the USA, so it would require a major marketing effort to persuade the American public to buy them. It would also require a major engineering and design effort to make the cars sufficiently attractive to sell in the quantities that the company needed.

The strategy was put into action from 1978. The first Mercedes diesel model for the USA was a version of the flagship S Class range. The idea was to use this car to give diesel power an upmarket and socially responsible image, and then to follow it with lower-powered and lower-priced diesel models. Most of these would be designed specifically for the USA and would not be made available in other countries. While this bold strategy enabled Mercedes to hold on to its reputation as a maker of well-engineered and prestigious cars, its engineers were beavering away back in Germany to develop the new small car that would improve the balance of its CAFE figures even more. That car was the W201.

It proved to be a successful strategy. By the time the W201 went on sale in North America, the nation's buyers were beginning to turn away from diesel power. Mercedes had, however, managed to build a strong following for its diesel models and so the new 190 range was made available with both petrol and diesel engines. The legacy of the holding operation that Mercedes had mounted in the USA would prove to be so strong that the company would continue to sell diesel-powered W201s alongside the petrol versions for the entire lifetime of the range.

THE FIRST AMERICAN W201s

The W201s, which quickly gained the affectionate nickname of 'Baby Benz' in the USA, were introduced in September 1983. This was some nine months after their launch in other markets – the intervening period had been used to complete work on the special US specification. In the beginning, the models sold in North America were unique to that market. Although some North American journalists had attended the launch of the European models in Spain at the end of 1982, there was a dedicated North American model launch in August 1983, based on the Greenbriar luxury resort in West Virginia. Those who attended also had a chance to try the cars out at the Indianapolis speedway track.

There were just two models at first, one with a petrol engine and one with a diesel engine. The petrol model was called a 190E 2.3 and the diesel was a 190D 2.2. As those names suggest, both of them had engines that were larger than the ones available in Europe. This was because meeting US emissions-control regulations reduced engine outputs,

and the simplest way of restoring the losses was to increase the swept volume of the engines.

The 2.2-litre diesel engine in the 190D 2.2 was simply a long-stroke derivative of the 2.0-litre OM601 in the European-specification 190D. Its 73PS was clearly comparable to the 72PS of a 190D, but it was actually developed at lower revs. Maximum torque was slightly higher, at the same engine speeds as in the 2.0-litre diesel. The extra 200cc compensated for the losses brought about by fitting an Exhaust Gas Recirculation (EGR) system, which was required under Californian emissions laws that had been adopted in eleven other western states of the USA.

From the start, the standard gearbox in a 190D 2.2 was a five-speed manual with overdrive top gear. Despite the axle gearing being lower than that used with the five-speed gearbox in the 190D (where it was an extra-cost option), the US cars were capable of returning between 40mpg and 50mpg (based on the US gallon, which is smaller than the Imperial gallon used in the UK; 5.9 to 4.7ltr/100km). The alternative gearbox was the same four-speed automatic as was optional in the 190D, again allied to lower final drive gearing. Acceleration and top speed with the manual gearbox were comparable with those of the European 190D, although the automatic 190D 2.2 was slower off the mark and had a lower top speed than the European car. Mercedes-Benz USA (MBUSA) used the new 190D 2.2 to replace the 240D version of the medium-sized 123-series saloons in its range, imports of the older car coming to an end with immediate effect. It was a good move: from the start, the 190D 2.2 accounted for a high 40 per cent of all diesel Mercedes cars sold in the USA each year.

As for the 190E 2.3, this special North American model had a petrol engine that was not available outside the USA and Canada. It was a large-bore relative of the 2.0-litre M102 four-cylinder seen in the European 190E, and more directly used the bore and stroke dimensions of the 2.3-litre M102 already in production for the 123-series 230E saloon. This engine, though, incorporated improvements made in preparing the smaller engine for the W201 range.

Despite its additional 202cc, the 2.3-litre engine was not as powerful as the

Keen to emphasize the handling qualities of the new 190 range when it was launched, MBUSA issued this publicity picture of a car leaning hard while cornering. The US-specification recessed headlamps are clear, but visually the car otherwise resembled its European equivalent very closely.

Built for the USA market alone was the 190D 2.2, which was the only diesel model available through MBUSA in the beginning. This picture shows its unique boot-lid badges. MR.CHOPPERS/WIKIMEDIA COMMONS

smaller engine in the European 190E. The combined effects of a lowered compression ratio (which at 8.0:1 was chosen to suit low-octane unleaded fuel) and a three-way catalytic converter in the exhaust system brought power down to 113bhp (roughly 114PS), which compared poorly with 122PS in the European car. Even a lower final drive ratio was only partial compensation, but US buyers for the most part did not know what they were missing. The car sold well with its standard five-speed overdrive gearbox (the ratios of which were slightly different from those in the diesel model) and optional four-speed automatic alternative.

Both the 190D 2.2 and the 190E 2.3 also looked quite different from their European equivalents. Fortunately, the standard bumpers had been designed to meet US low-speed impact regulations, so there was no need for the ugly extended bumpers that had ruined the appearance of some earlier Mercedes models sold in the USA. However, the W201s did have to have special headlights in order to meet US regulations. Cars were required to use one of a small number of standardized headlights, so that replacements were readily available across the nation and owners would not have to search for an outlet dedicated to a par-

ticular marque. The W201s therefore had special light units, with the foglight in its standard position but the headlight replaced by a removable rectangular sealed-beam unit. This was set back from the front face of the light unit. There was a consequent negative effect on aerodynamics, so US W201s always had a higher drag coefficient than their European equivalents. The light output from the sealed-beam units was also inferior to that of the European halogen types.

American buyers also tended to order their cars with more electrical options than was common in Europe at the time; air conditioning and electric windows were just two of the items that were far more common on North American W201s. As a result, the North American cars were fitted as a matter of course with a 910-watt alternator instead of the 770-watt type that was standard in Europe. Uphol-stery options were nevertheless the same as in Europe: the cars could be ordered with MB-Tex vinyl, velour or leather, according to taste. In addition, of course, every new W201 sold in the USA through official channels came with the company's usual five-year/50,000-mile warranty and a national Roadside Assistance programme with a dedicated free telephone number.

THE 1985 MODELS

All the first W201s for the USA were of course 1984 models. While they were on sale, the company was taking careful note of customer feedback and working on improvements for the future. They were well aware from early on that the performance of the 113bhp 190E 2.3 was disappointing, so by the start of the new model-year in autumn 1984 they had developed the engine to deliver 120bhp (122PS), which was the same as the European 2.0-litre type in the 190E. The extra power came from a new camshaft and from modifications to the inlet manifold and the injection system.

This would be the last year for the 190D 2.2, which lost a certain amount of power (the exact figure is unclear) thanks to new emissions laws. For 1985, all states in the USA now required diesel cars to have a ceramic particulates filter (usually known as a diesel particulates filter, or DPF) in the exhaust system. All the 1985 models for North America now had ABS as standard, and there was a new optional safety package that combined a driver's airbag with an automatic belt tensioner for the front passenger. Recognizing that some drivers would choose not to wear a seat belt, Mercedes also added a cushioned knee bolster under the left-hand side of the dashboard. This helped to restrain the driver's body in an accident and meant that he or she would not submarine under the airbag.

PRESS REACTION TO THE 190D 2.2 AND 190E 2.3

When *Car & Driver* magazine reported their initial driving impressions of a five-speed 190E 2.3 in the November 1983 issue, they also succinctly summarized pre-launch US attitudes to the new compact Mercedes. These are worth repeating here.

'There was an initial irritation expressed in the automotive community when rumors about the baby Merc surfaced,' they said. 'Where did those Germans get off thinking they could dump a $24,000 Honda Accord replica on the American public? .... In short, the 190s came to this shore cloaked in more scepticism than any other Stuttgart products since the first post-war 170s.'

However, that first drive by *Car & Driver* left an impression that completely validated all Mercedes' efforts in crafting the W201 range: 'Now we have seen and driven the cars, and the tune has changed.... These are... a meticulously crafted new breed of Mercedes [that] present the impres-

North American models came as standard with Mercedes' SRS system, which consisted of a driver's airbag and a belt-tensioning system for both front seats. The airbag steering wheel had a rather unprepossessing appearance. Like all North American cars that had a manual gearbox, this one has a five-speed type. It also has a speedometer marked in kilometres per hour, which suggests it was probably destined for Canada.

sion that they have been hand-carved out of an ingot of chrome-molybdenum steel.' The magazine's Brock Yates added, 'This wasn't a new automobile so much as a perfect seven-eighths-scale model of the acclaimed S class cars.' Rich Ceppos chimed in with his view that 'there is a greatness in this car, just as there has been in every Merc that's come down the Autobahn'.

Perfect it was not, although in many areas it came close: 'The Mercedes' controls initially felt a bit rubbery, and its shift linkage, while silky in the extreme, tended to shroud the gates into third and fifth.' The car also tended to understeer: 'In our opinion, and in the opinion of some insiders at Mercedes-Benz of North America, the car needs lower-profile tires regardless of the penalties in aerodynamic drag and fuel mileage.'

On the press launch, the PR team offered various prizes for the long drive between the Greenbriar resort and the Indianapolis speedway that had been hired for high-speed testing. The *Car & Driver* team were first home: 'We arrived 35 minutes ahead of the second-place finisher and averaged a rather decent 64.5mph for the journey, but our 24mpg fuel consumption was sufficiently miserable to garner us the Friends of OPEC award at the final ceremonies. One team got as much as 40mpg with their 190E... [and] the winning diesel number for the trip was 41mpg.' Testing against the stopwatch produced a 10.1-second time for the 0–60mph sprint.

Car & Driver, however, was clearly not a fan of diesel cars. 'The diesel is a diesel,' they wrote. 'Nothing more, nothing less. It is superbly quiet and well mannered as the breed goes, but it remains a curiosity for cranks who perhaps shouldn't be reading this magazine in the first place.'

There was no doubt that the car was a triumph, although the magazine did mention indications that other manufacturers, especially from Japan, were catching up with the traditional excellence of Mercedes products. That closing of the traditional gap became glaringly apparent a couple of years later when *Road & Track* magazine compared a 190E 2.3 with the latest Honda Accord SE-i, which had a 101bhp 1.8-litre engine and cost just $13,000, or $10,000 less than the Mercedes.

The magazine confirmed the now fairly universal view that the 'smaller-than-usual Mercedes [was] every bit a Mercedes'. Their car was once again a 190E 2.3 with five-speed gearbox, but with the more powerful engine that had been introduced in autumn 1985. They were less than impressed: 'The Mercedes engine throbs inappropriately for a $23,000 car and is so short on low-speed torque that it needs to be driven rather hard.' They were not keen on the gearbox, either: '[It] isn't state-of-the-art. The linkage makes a clunking sound when moved from one gear to the next, feels less than precise and sometimes balks when you're trying to downshift into 2nd or 1st.'

Despite the prestige and status associated with the Mercedes, and despite its traditional qualities, it was certainly not unfair to compare it with the very much cheaper Honda. 'All four testers voted the Mercedes their choice if cost were no object,' the magazine concluded. But, when price was taken into consideration, 'all chose the Honda'.

1986

A Bigger Diesel

With power in the petrol model already increased – although not by very much – North American customers

The 190D 2.2 gave way to the five-cylinder 190D 2.5 in summer 1985. This publicity picture was clearly intended to suggest that the car had good performance – with 90PS, that was stretching the imagination a little!

The Cosworth-engined car was made available to North American customers in limited numbers. With the SRS system as standard, it also had the US-specification headlights and, of course, a catalytic converter that robbed the engine of a little power.

known as a CHMSL (centre, high-mounted stop lamp), was mounted behind the rear screen, just above the parcels shelf.

A 190E 2.3-16 for North America

No doubt with the aim of stealing a march on BMW, Mercedes announced a North American version of the 190E 2.3-16 in March 1986. Inevitably, it was not quite as quick as its European equivalent: the extra drag of those American-specification headlights and the power losses in its emissions-controlled engine saw to that. With its compression ratio reduced to 9.7:1 and a catalytic converter as standard, the engine nevertheless boasted 167bhp (170PS), and lower axle gearing made sure the manual-gearbox car could despatch the 0–60mph increment in a little under 7.5 seconds.

Mercedes allocated just 1,880 examples of the car for North America, although the split between five-speed manual and four-speed automatic models is not known. At a whisker under $35,000, the car instantly became the most expensive W201 variant on sale in North America by a considerable margin. Yet there seems to have been no difficulty in finding owners who were willing to find the necessary cash, and in many cases to add a few options as well. All models sold in the USA of course had the driver's airbag and passenger's belt pre-tensioner that were now standard right across the North American Mercedes range. They came with leather upholstery (there was no cloth option) and the console-mounted stopwatch, and they also had a neat CHMSL embedded in the centre support of the tail spoiler.

BMW hit back with a North American version of the M3, but it did not go on sale until summer 1987. By then, all the Cosworth Mercedes were long gone from dealers' showrooms.

were offered a more powerful diesel model for the 1986 season. This was the 190D 2.5, the five-cylinder model that had also entered production for Europe in May 1985. Obviously, using the same engine for Europe and North America reduced manufacturing costs for Mercedes, and the 190D 2.2 now disappeared completely, with the last examples being built in August 1985. The new model went on sale in October.

The North American 190D 2.5 was not quite the same as its European equivalent, of course. With 90PS at 4,600rpm, its engine power remained unchanged, despite the presence of EGR equipment, but the car was given much taller axle ratios than its European equivalent. With the standard five-speed manual gearbox, it had a 3.42:1 ratio that contrasted with the European ratio of 3.64:1; and with the automatic option, the axle ratio was 3.07:1 instead of the European 3.24:1. Presumably, these figures had been chosen to improve fuel consumption and so contribute towards the Mercedes CAFE figures; they certainly reduced the accelerative performance of the car.

From the start of the 1986 calendar-year, all the North American W201s were further modified with a third brake lamp from the start of 1986, which satisfied new legislation that came into force at that time. The extra lamp, often

Press Reaction to the 190E 2.3-16

Motor Trend magazine secured an early test drive of a 2.3-16 and published the result in its March 1986 issue. It had no reservations about the car's overall performance: 'Judged by either the fifth wheel or the seat of your pants, the 2.3-16 is very quick. It springs from 0 to 60 in only 7.3 seconds… [and] top speed rises to a stable 134mph.' The reviewer was also very impressed by the handling: 'At 0.80g on the skidpad, the 2.3-16 is the hardest-cornering stock Benz we have tested, ranking well up among today's finest sedans.'

Fuel economy was not the car's strong suit. The five-speed model managed only 18mpg (13.1ltr/100km), using Super Unleaded petrol measured in small American gallons. There were also some niggles about its controls: 'The clutch action is lumpy, and there's a clunk at the end of the engagement very much reminiscent of the little jolt that BMWs have emitted for years… Though we prefer the more conventional [gate] pattern, this transmission is certainly light to the touch… Still, we wonder whether the automatic might be a better intermediary between the power and the pavement.'

Acknowledging that the 16-valve car was very different from the Mercedes that US buyers were used to, the magazine nevertheless wondered whether a more traditional model might do the same job just as well. 'The slick new mid-sized 300E sedan is a tempting alternative. It costs a thousand dollars less than this wee scrapper, and it could well be a better car for most buyers.'

When *Road & Track* tested a manual-gearbox model for its August 1986 issue, it found the 2.3-16 'an impressive car overall'. 'It's relatively exclusive, looks right, and handles and stops well.' Its brakes were 'right up there with the best we've ever tested' and, overall, this was 'one of the tastiest four-doors in the world'. Surprisingly, perhaps, the main criticism was levelled at its engine. The testers felt that it did not have 'as much torque as some drivers have come to expect, and it has to be revved to develop decent power'. They concluded that the car was certainly 'not for everyone'. Like *Motor Trend*, *Road & Track* wondered whether a 300E would be a better buy, and listed the larger Mercedes among cars with 'similar or better attributes'.

1987: TURBOS AND SIXES

Turbos

The 1986 model-year had seen the North American W201

Just visible in the rear window of this 1987 190E 2.3 is the CHMSL (third brake light) that became standard on US-model W201s at the start of 1986. IFCAR/WIKIMEDIA COMMONS

range grow to three models: the 190D 2.5, 190E 2.3 and 190E 2.3-16. For 1987, there would be a fourth model, the 190D 2.5 Turbo; and then, at about the mid-point of the 1987 model-year, the 190E 2.3 would be replaced by another new model, the 190E 2.6.

By this stage, Mercedes had begun to close the gap between the European and North American specifications for its W201 range. The new West German requirement for catalytic converters actually simplified things, because it brought the specifications of the petrol models closer together. Meanwhile, the need to provide desirable diesel models for the North American market drove development of these, with European customers reaping the benefits as well.

From spring 1986, the new turbocharged 190D 2.5 Turbo model demonstrated quite clearly what was happening. For the 1987 model-year, North America received very much the same car as the Europeans. Both had an engine with 122PS, but the North American car could be had with the alternatives of a five-speed (standard) or automatic (optional) gearbox, whereas all the European cars were automatic. Axle gearing was the same. North American cars had the special headlamps used in that market and came with the driver's airbag and seat-belt tensioners as standard. These were an extra-cost option for Europe.

Sixes

The differences between North American and European versions of the next new model were once again minimal, but the six-cylinder 190E 2.6 that became available in the USA from April 1987 had a special function in the North American line-up. In Europe, the 2.6-litre car simply became the top-of-the-range model; in North America, it became the only petrol W201 on sale, replacing the four-cylinder 190E 2.3.

On the mechanical side, the six-cylinder car shared its basic specification with the KAT versions introduced for Europe a year earlier. Its M103 engine put out 160PS (158bhp in American figures) and developed 220Nm (162 lb ft) of torque at 4,600rpm on a 9.2:1 compression ratio. A five-speed overdrive manual gearbox was standard and the well-proven four-speed automatic was an extra-cost option. Unsurprisingly, MBUSA had seized the opportunity to raise the showroom price. The 190E 2.3 had last been listed at $29,190; the new six-cylinder car that replaced it

was expected to cost $31,590 with the five-speed gearbox and $35,500 with the automatic option.

By the end of the 1987 model-year, in summer 1987, the North American W201 line-up consisted of four models. The petrol types were the 190E 2.6 and the 190E 2.3-16, although in practice very few examples of the Cosworth car remained unsold. The diesel types were the 190D 2.5 and the 190D 2.5 Turbo. The line-up would now remain unchanged for a further year, with the 190E 2.6 generally being seen as a model that was new for the 1988 season.

Press Reaction to the 190E 2.6

By the time US magazines came to try the 190E 2.6, the fact that the W201 was a compact saloon and the smallest of the Mercedes range no longer really mattered. It had been fully accepted as a Mercedes, and as typical of the maker's products.

Nevertheless, *Car & Driver* did pick up on the limited interior space when they tried an automatic example for their April 1987 issue. The latest encroachment on space from the driver's knee bolster particularly came in for adverse comment. Their view was that the car was superbly constructed: 'True to tradition, the quality of the 190E, inside and out, is past great and headed for awesome.' It was also formidably expensive, however, with a base price quoted by the magazine of $32,200. This was the East Coast price, which would be further inflated by shipping costs for West Coast buyers.

Most of the comment was of course focused on the new engine, which was deemed to '[compare] well with the most potent two-valve-per-cylinder motors from anywhere in the world.' It delivered on the promise of its extra capacity: 'You expect brisk performance and you get it, with 60mph arriving 8.1 seconds after liftoff and the quarter-mile going by in 16.4 seconds at a racy 84mph.... Around town there is always plenty of torque on call when you need to squirt ahead of traffic.' In other circumstances, 'it settles back to a well-oiled hum when you're just cruising. An enthusiast could live on the sound alone.'

West Coast-based *Automobile* magazine went to Germany to test a European-specification automatic, but accompanied their feature in the May 1987 issue with photographs of a Californian-specification car. They were full of praise for the car: 'If you have a chance to drive, or own, the 190E 2.6, grab it. Take it from one who usually doesn't like Mercedes

For 1989, the US models were facelifted in the same way as those for other markets, but of course they retained their special front light units. IFCAR/WIKIMEDIA COMMONS

automobiles: it's splendid.' This model, they claimed in the headline of their feature, was 'the connoisseur's 190'.

Comparing the six-cylinder car with a four-cylinder European 190E driven immediately before it, *Automobile* found that 'all the noise and vibration, the all but imperceptible amount there is in the four, was gone'. They were also of the opinion that, when subjected to some more energetic driving, the car was 'never untidy, and at anything other than racetrack speeds, it will always understeer ever so slightly, without any of the sudden change of character *in extremis* that so mars many other German cars'.

1989: THE FACELIFT

In autumn 1988, the North American 201s were facelifted in the same way as their European counterparts. The 190E 2.6, 190D 2.5 and 190D 2.5 Turbo all gained the plastic flank panels and interior improvements made for 1989. Noticeable in its absence from the 1989 range, however, was the latest 2.5-litre version of the 16-valve Cosworth car. Exactly why this was not made available for North America is not clear, but there were probably two factors at play. One would have been the cost of developing a North American version that would sell only in limited numbers. The other may have been that the fuel economy of the Cosworth car was poor enough to cause difficulties with the CAFE figures

– the earlier 2.3-16 had typically returned around 18mpg (13.1ltr/100km), which was unimpressive.

However, sales of the W201 had peaked in North America in the 1986 model-year. They had gradually declined since then, and while the 1989 facelift may have slowed the decline, it was not able to reverse it. The sales total dropped a little further during the 1990 calendar-year, despite the introduction of another new model in the autumn.

THE 1991 MODEL-YEAR

Reprising the Four-Cylinder 190E 2.3

The 'new' model that MBUSA introduced in autumn 1990 for the 1991 model-year was not quite new. It was actually a reprise of the four-cylinder 190E 2.3 that had been replaced by the 190E 2.6 back in 1987. Sliding sales were probably one reason for its re-introduction. However, it was also true that North America's love affair with diesel cars was by now just a memory, and Mercedes needed to offer more than one petrol-engined version of the W201 if the car was to retain its position in the market.

The 1991-model 190E 2.3 retained the name of the model discontinued in 1987, but it was actually a very different car in many ways. For a start, it came with all the features of the facelifted cars that had been introduced for 1989. Per-

In the evening sunlight, the silver paint on this 1991-model 190E 2.6 turns a golden colour, and the dark grey flank panels provide a strong contrast. Again, the CHMSL is just visible through the rear window, above the parcels shelf.

introduced to the US market nearly eight years ago.' The handling was also not entirely competitive, despite the high level of ride comfort. 'Everyone marvelled at the velvety suppleness of the 190E's ride – a distinct change from the firmness of Mercedes-Benz cars of just a few years ago… [but] its roll softness, slow-reacting recirculating-ball steering and [narrow] tires … made trying to keep up with the better-handling cars [in the test group] a challenge.'

The extra power of the newly uprated engine did not occasion comment, but *Road & Track* did highlight a certain lack of refinement: '[The engine] vibrates noticeably at idle… [but] smooths out quite nicely and soldiers authoritatively up to its 6000rpm redline.' On the other hand, 'the 5-speed's shift linkage is reasonably precise and delicate-feeling, with a satisfying way of springing out of one gear and into the next (when you intentionally move the lever, that is)'. The magazine recorded 11.4 seconds for the 0–60mph time but (as was the fashion at the time) did not offer a maximum speed figure.

haps more importantly, it was also noticeably more powerful than its earlier incarnation. That car had 113bhp (114PS), whereas the new model came with 130bhp (132PS), which was the same as had been standard for the European 190E 2.3 since autumn 1988. The 190E 2.3 also allowed Mercedes to lower the entry-level price for ownership of a W201 in the USA; the base price was now $28,350 for the standard car with five-speed manual gearbox and, as before, a four-speed automatic was optional at extra cost.

Press Reaction to the 190E 2.3

'The 190E has aged gracefully through the years; it's comforting that substance and understated elegance never seem to go out of style,' said *Road & Track* magazine in their August 1991 report on the re-introduced 190E 2.3. This was a standard five-speed model, the least expensive Mercedes then available in the USA, but, according to *Road & Track*, 'cut-rate pricing doesn't mean skimping on quality; much of what makes the S class sedans so desirable is present in the 190E 2.3'.

This was a comparison test with competitive models, all of them considerably newer than the 190. Unsurprisingly, then, the styling did not get a thumbs-up: 'Both inside and out, [it] is conservative and a constant reminder that the 190E was

THE 1992 AND 1993 MODEL-YEARS

An economic recession during 1991 affected sales of all cars in the USA, and sales of the W201 range were certainly adversely affected. Although sales bounced back a little for 1992, they were still below the levels seen in the mid-1980s, and for 1993 they would drop again.

The model line-up remained unchanged during the last two years of W201 production. There were two petrol models (the 190E 2.3 and 190E 2.6) and two diesel models (the 190D 2.5 and 190D 2.5 Turbo). Five-speed manual gearboxes were standard on all of them, with the four-speed automatic an extra-cost option. Traditionally, the automatic gearbox had started from rest in second gear unless deliberately kicked down; for 1992, it was modified to start in first gear, which gave the impression that the cars were a little quicker than before.

The 1992 models were also prewired for a portable phone and had a CD changer in the boot as standard. A headlight wash-wipe system was now made standard, along with an anti-theft alarm. Perhaps the most interesting of the changes for the 1992 model-year was the availability of the Sportline option, which had been introduced as long ago as 1989 in Europe but had not so far made it to North America. As on the European cars, it brought a lowered ride height, stiffer springs and dampers, more direct steering with a smaller steering wheel, and wider (205/55 R 15) tyres. The more supportive seats came too, as did identifying badges on the plastic panels of the front wings. Typically, the Sportline package was ordered for the top-of-the-range 190E 2.6 models, but it may be that some lesser models also had it to individual order.

The 1993 model-year would be the last one for the W201 in North America, as it was in Europe. The replacement C Class W202 models were scheduled to go on sale in November 1993, and MBUSA made sure that the last of the 190s had gone from the showrooms by providing a buyer's incentive in the shape of two limited editions.

These run-out editions were both based on the petrol models, while the diesels were left to fend for themselves. There were 700 examples of the 190E 2.3 specially finished in Emerald Green with Cream leather upholstery, and the

MERCEDES-BENZ 190 US SALES	
Figures are for calendar-years	
1983	6,122
1984	19,548
1985	12,978
1986	21,897
1987	17,619
1988	16,945
1989	14,677
1990	14,344
1991	13,923
1992	15,966
1993	14,772

same number of 190E 2.6 models available only in Black, with Black leather upholstery. Both had eight-hole alloy wheels, automatic climate control, Burr Walnut wood trim and electric seats. And with those, the W201 disappeared from North American showrooms.

Not part of a known limited edition, but apparently painted in the Azzurro Blue associated with those for other countries, this is a late model 190D 2.5.

TECHNICAL SPECIFICATIONS: MERCEDES-BENZ W201 MODELS FOR THE US MARKET

Engine (190E 2.3)

M102 four-cylinder with cast-iron block and alloy cylinder head
2299cc (95.5mm bore × 80.25mm stroke)
Single overhead camshaft, two valves per cylinder
Five-bearing crankshaft
Compression ratio 8.0:1
Bosch KE-Jetronic mechanical fuel injection
Catalytic converter in exhaust
Max. power 113bhp (114PS) at 5,000rpm
Max. torque 133lb ft (181Nm) at 3,500rpm

Compression ratio 9.0:1
Bosch KE-Jetronic mechanical fuel injection
Catalytic converter in exhaust
Max. power 130bhp (132PS) at 5,100rpm
Max. torque 146lb ft (198Nm) at 3,500rpm

Engine (190E 2.3-16)

M102 four-cylinder with cast-iron block and alloy cylinder head
2299cc (95mm bore × 80.25mm stroke)
Two overhead camshafts, four valves per cylinder
Five-bearing crankshaft
Compression ratio 9.7:1
Bosch KE-Jetronic mechanical fuel injection
Max. power 170PS at 5,800rpm
Max. torque 220Nm at 4,750rpm

Engine (190E 2.6)

M103 six-cylinder with cast-iron block and alloy cylinder head
2599cc (82.9mm bore × 80.25mm stroke)
Single overhead camshaft, two valves per cylinder
Four-bearing crankshaft
Compression ratio 9.2:1

Bosch KE-Jetronic mechanical fuel injection
Max. power 160PS at 5,800rpm
Max. torque 220Nm at 4,600rpm

Engine (190D 2.2)

OM601 four-cylinder diesel with cast-iron block and alloy cylinder head
2197cc (87mm bore × 92.4mm stroke)
Single overhead camshaft, two valves per cylinder
Five-bearing crankshaft
Compression ratio 22:1
Indirect injection with Bosch pump
Exhaust Gas Recirculation
Max. power 73PS at 4,200rpm
Max. torque 130Nm at 2,800rpm

Engine (190D 2.5)

OM602 five-cylinder with cast-iron block and alloy cylinder head
2497cc (87mm bore × 84mm stroke)
Single overhead camshaft, two valves per cylinder
Six-bearing crankshaft
Compression ratio 22:1
Indirect injection with Bosch pump
Exhaust Gas Recirculation
Max. power 90PS at 4,600rpm
Max. torque 154Nm at 2,800rpm

Engine (190D 2.5 Turbo)

OM602 five-cylinder with cast-iron block and alloy cylinder head
2497cc (87mm bore × 84mm stroke)
Single overhead camshaft, two valves per cylinder
Six-bearing crankshaft
Compression ratio 22:1
Indirect injection with Bosch pump and turbocharger
Exhaust Gas Recirculation
Max. power 122PS at 4,600rpm
Max. torque 225Nm at 2,400rpm

Gearbox
Five-speed manual GL68/20 B-5 (190E 2.3, 190D 2.5)
    Ratios 3.91:1, 2.17:1, 1.37:1, 1.00:1, 0.78:1, reverse 4.27:1
Five-speed manual GL68/20 A-5 (190D 2.2)
    Ratios 4.23:1, 2.36:1, 1.49:1, 1.00:1, 0.84:1, reverse 4.63:1
Five-speed manual GL76/27 F-5 (190E 2.6)
    Ratios 3.86:1, 2.18:1, 1.38:1, 1.00:1, 0.80:1, reverse 4.22:1
Five-speed close-ratio manual (190E 2.3-16)
    Ratios 4.08:1, 2.52:1, 1.77:1, 1.26:1, 1.00:1, reverse 4.16:1
Four-speed automatic W4A 020 (190E 2.3, 190E 2.3-16, 190E
    2.6, 190D 2.2, 190D 2.5, 190D 2.5 Turbo)
    Ratios 4.25:1, 2.41:1, 1.49:1, 1.00:1, reverse 5.67:1
    Torque converter multiplication 2.2

Axle ratio
2.65:1 (190D 2.5 Turbo)
3.07:1 (190E 2.6 automatic, 190D 2.5 automatic)
3.27:1 (190E 2.3, 190E 2.3-16, 190E 2.6 five-speed)
3.42:1 (190D 2.2)
3.64:1 (190D 2.5 five-speed)

Suspension
Front suspension with MacPherson struts, wishbones, coil springs, telescopic gas dampers and anti-roll bar; adjustable ride height optional on 190E 2.3-16.
Rear suspension with five links, coil springs, telescopic gas dampers and anti-roll bar; hydro-pneumatic self-levelling strut standard on 190E 2.3-16 and optional on other models.

Steering
Recirculating-ball steering with power assistance.

Brakes
Disc brakes on all four wheels, ventilated at the front on 190E 2.3-16 and 190E 2.6; dual hydraulic circuit and servo assistance; ABS optional on 1984 models and standard from 1985 model-year.

Dimensions
Overall length: 4,420mm
    4,430mm for 190E 2.3-16
    4,448mm from 1989 model-year
Overall width: 1,678 mm
    1,690mm from 1989 model-year
    1,706mm for 190E 2.3-16
Overall height: 1,390mm
    1,375mm from 1989 model-year
    1,353mm with Sportline option
    1,361mm for 190E 2.3-16
Wheelbase: 2,665mm
Track, front: 1,428mm to December 1984
    1,437mm from January 1985
    1,441mm from 1989 model-year
    1,445mm for 190E 2.3-16
Track, rear: 1,415mm to December 1984
    1,418mm from January 1985
    1,421mm from 1989 model-year
    1,429mm for 190E 2.3-16

Wheels and tyres
6J × 15 steel disc wheels with 175/70 R 14 tyres, to December 1984
6J × 15 alloy wheels with 175/70 R 14 tyres optional
6J × 15 steel disc wheels with 185/65 R 15 tyres from January 1985
6J × 15 alloy wheels with 185/65 R 15 tyres optional
7J × 15 alloy wheels with 205/55 VR 15 tyres, for 190E 2.3-16 and Sportline option

Running weight
190E 2.3: 1,190kg (1,220kg from 1991 model-year)
190E 2.3-16: 1,260kg
190E 2.6: 1,220kg
190D 2.2: 1,200kg
190D 2.5: 1,175kg (1,230kg from 1989 model-year)
190D 2.5 Turbo: 1,250kg

CHAPTER SEVEN

GLORY DAYS

There was never any doubt that Mercedes intended the 190E 2.3-16 to be competitive in motor racing, but they held back from committing themselves to a racing programme. There was no 'works' team; instead, the company took a very cautious approach, leaving the actual racing to others. The 2.3-16 was homologated in 1985 under FIA Group A rules (which required a minimum of 5,000 road cars to be built), but Mercedes declined at this stage to supply cars with the permitted modifications. Their support for privateers

went no further than providing details of those permitted modifications. Nevertheless, it would not be long before the W201 made its mark in touring car racing

From the later 1980s Mercedes gave official support to a number of teams in the DTM (German Touring Car Championship). Although the DTM was not the only series in which W201 raced, it became central to the story of the cars, so this chapter focuses on the Mercedes DTM programme and does not cover the other events.

It's never over until it's over: Kurt Thiim and his 1991 mount were reunited for a demonstration event in 2016.

1985: A TENTATIVE START

Homologation was achieved on 1 May 1985, in the month when the 5,000th car was built. Permitted modifications were more direct steering, modified brakes and different gear ratios, centre-lock wheels and some aluminium body panels. The May date was rather late for any teams to prepare cars for the 1985 racing season, but within a month Hartmann Motorsport had a car ready for privateer Leopold Gallina to race in the Deutsche Produktionswagen Meisterschaft (DPM, or German Production Car Championship). Although Gallina did not have a good season – he failed to start at the Mainz-Finthen round in June and did not finish at any of the other three rounds he entered – he remained undeterred. He would be back with the Mercedes for 1986.

Meanwhile, Snobeck Racing Service in France also seized on the newly available car, switching from the Alfa Romeo Alfetta with which Dany Snobeck had won the 1984 French Touring Car Championship. For 1985, Snobeck and regular team driver Alain Cudini campaigned a pair of cars that the team had developed to produce around 240PS from the standard production 185PS. Sponsorship came from Mercedes-Benz France and from various dealers.

The Snobeck team was based at the Magny-Cours racing circuit, with good access to testing facilities. It did well in that year's French Touring Car Championship, although the cars suffered their fair share of problems with oil pressure, clutches and axles. This was, after all, the first season for the Mercedes in competition and there was as yet no well of experience or of special parts on which the French team could draw. Nevertheless, Cudini finished the season in third place behind the winning Rover Vitesse of Jean-Louis Schlesser and the second-placed BMW 635 CSi of Xavier Lapeyre. Snobeck finished in fourth place. It was a most encouraging start for the new Mercedes.

1986: THE FIRST DTM ENTRIES

For 1986, the DPM was reorganized and rebranded as the DTM (Deutsche Tourenwagen Meisterschaft, or German Touring Car Championship). The success of the Snobeck team during 1985 had persuaded several more private teams to take a look at the new Mercedes, and 1986 would see entries in the European Touring Car Championship, too, from Snobeck, the Carlsson team and others. However, it was the DTM that would become the focus for the Mer-

Frenchman Dany Snobeck was a pioneer in racing the W201, and would eventually drive cars for a team supported by the Mercedes factory. This picture was taken in 2012. ELTONY007/WIKIMEDIA COMMONS

cedes, and over the next few years it would offer some of the most exciting touring car racing ever seen as manufacturers took an interest. In particular, the duels between the Mercedes entries and the BMW M3 would provide some memorable moments, but they were by no means alone in doing so: there were also strong entries from Ford (Sierras, and later the RS500 Cosworth), Opel (the Omega) and Volvo (the 240 Turbo).

The 1986 season saw participation from AMG, the leading aftermarket tuner of Mercedes cars, who prepared two cars for the Marko RSM team from Austria. At the start of the season, these were driven by Franz Klammer (the Austrian ski champion) and Peter Oberndorfer. After three rounds, Volker Weidler replaced Oberndorfer, who then joined rival team Scuderia Kassel, where he again drove a 16-valve Mercedes. The Marko cars ran as numbers 8 (Oberndorfer or Weidler) and 9 (Klammer).

Scuderia Kassel also fielded a pair of 16-valve Mercedes. Number 33 was driven by Johannes Breuer or Jörg van

The 16-valve engine had originally been developed for motorsport use, and the road cars used heavily detuned versions. One of the DTM race engines is pictured here at an exhibition in Prague in 2018. (JIŘÍ SEDLÁČEK/WIKIMEDIA COMMONS)

Ommen, and number 64 was shared by the Danish driver Kris Nissen, Sepp Haider and, after he joined the team in July, Peter Oberndorfer. A fifth Mercedes in the championship was entered by the determined Leopold Gallina.

The Mercedes were running on 16-inch Ronal rims in this season, with a regulation racing weight of 1,010kg. Typically making around 240PS, the engines gave considerable trouble in the first round of the championship, but the teams soon got on top of this, leaving suspension as the area most in need of development. From the start, the Marko team cars in particular showed considerable promise. In May there was a Mercedes 1-2 finish at the Avus track in Berlin, where Volker Weidler won for the Marko team and Johannes Breuer came second for Scuderia Kassel. The most telling sign of the Mercedes' success, however, was the clamour from rival teams for the cars to run with a weight penalty – a request that was turned down by the event organizers.

By mid-season, the Mercedes had become the cars to beat. By the end, Volker Weidler had earned enough points to take second place behind the well-established Rover Vitesse of Kurt Thiim. Even more telling was the regular sight in the paddock of Mercedes factory representatives, showing an intense interest in what the privateers were achieving with the 190E 2.3-16.

1987: SERIOUSLY CHALLENGED

Mercedes kept an even closer eye on the ten rounds of the 1987 DTM, where the introduction of the new BMW

M3 made the competition much more intense. The first round fell to Harald Grohs in the Bavarian constructor's new model, which was an indication of things to come, and the Belgian driver Eric van der Poele was declared winner at the end of the season with his Zakspeed BMW M3.

There was serious competition from the Fords as well, the XR4 Ti models used in the early rounds later giving way to the Sierra Cosworth. But the Mercedes, now on 17-inch wheels and typically running with 260PS at 7,750rpm, were simply not competitive, despite some sound results that ensured they were not totally outclassed.

The Marko RSM team this year entered three cars: number 11 for Jörg van Ommen, number 12 for Franz Klammer and number 13 for new driver Heiner Weiss. Their best results were van Ommen's third place at the opening round in Hockenheim and fourth at the second round in Zolder. Sachs Sporting fielded car number 32 for Jürgen Weiler, Format Fahrzeugteile had car number 29 for Ludwig Weber, Leopold Gallina entered again, now with car number 28, and Peter Oberndorfer tried his luck with a privately entered

Mercedes at the Norisring round in June. There were also single-round Mercedes entries by Costas Los, Stanley Dickens and Andreas Mark, but none made any real impression.

An interesting season closer was a non-championship eleventh round at Hockenheim in October, which was run as a trial of the planned 1988 DTM rules. It attracted an entry from Snobeck Racing Services, but Dany Snobeck's Mercedes did not finish, being put out of contention by a valve failure.

1988: THE FIRST WORKS TEAMS

The provocation from BMW in the shape of the M3 was too much for Mercedes and, well before the start of the 1988 racing season, the company had decided that it would provide support for teams running in that year's DTM. Over the winter of 1987–1988, the company worked with Snobeck Racing Service in France to develop a core specification for the 1988 2.3-16 racers, but the deal was that it would then leave the individual teams to develop the cars as they saw

Mercedes provided formal support for DTM teams running W201s for the first time in 1988. This is driver Roland Asch, driving for BMK Motorsport at the Bergischer Löwe race in Zolder, on 3 March 1988.

**Johnny Cecotto, who would later become
very successful with the BMW M3, pictured
here during the 1988 season, when he drove
car number 44 for the AMG team.**

fit. Meanwhile, they worked with AMG on developing the engine, with their own engineer Gerhard Lepler leading the development team and the cars being tested by driver Roland Asch.

As a result, the Mercedes cars that competed in the 1988 DTM ran on Speedline wheels instead of the earlier Ronal types. Power assistance for the steering had been dispensed with, and the cars had improved brake cooling and front brakes taken from the Mercedes Group C Sports Prototype programme. The DTM authorities allowed engine changes that went beyond the FIA Group A rules, which made the Mercedes far more competitive with the BMW M3s. Engine power was now up to 300PS at 8,500rpm and peak torque of 270Nm was generated at 7,000rpm. Acceleration from 0–100km/h was in the order of 5.2 seconds, although on the race tracks it was at much higher speeds that the improved acceleration was most useful.

Mercedes was not the only manufacturer to offer full works support this year, as BMW, Ford and Opel also backed the teams that fielded their cars. Among the sixteen drivers who campaigned the racing 16-valve Mercedes were three determined one-man privateers; the other thirteen owed their allegiance to five works-supported teams. These were AMG, BMK Motorsport, IPS Motorsport (from Sweden), Marko RSM (from Austria) and Snobeck Racing Service (from France).

Marko RSM once again fielded two cars for their regular drivers: number 15 for Jörg van Ommen and number 16 for Franz Klammer. Snobeck Racing Service were represented by Dany Snobeck in car number 27, Alain Cudini in car number 28 and Jean-Pierre Malcher in car number 29. Leopold Gallina once again entered with his own car, numbered 52.

Leading the newcomers was AMG (now an official partner of Mercedes-Benz), with no fewer than five cars. These were for drivers Kurt Thiim (car number 31), Johnny Cecotto (44), Marc Hessel (45), Heiner Weiss (46) and Jean-Louis Schlesser (65). Three cars were entered under the name of BMK Motorsport. Roland Asch in car number 41 also billed himself as Asch Motorsport, having bought his own car and decided to enter just three weeks before the first round of the season. The other two were Norbert Brenner (car 42) and Ralf-Werner Müller (car 43). IPS Motorsport had two cars, for Per Stureson (number 10) and Siegfried Müller Jr (number 12), and there was a single car for Schwaben Motorsport, which entered number 17 for Thomas von Löwis of Menar. Privateers Bob Wollek in car number 47 and Ludwig Weber in car 53 completed the ranks of Mercedes entries.

Not only were this year's regulations different from before, the format of each of the DTM's twelve rounds also changed; now, there were to be two heats. The cars also had to run on unleaded fuel, in line with West Germany's stance on air pollution. As the season progressed, so the Mercedes got better and better, although the turbocharged Sierras quickly became the cars to beat. Their progress was slowed only when the organizers reduced their advantage by insisting on restricting the size of their air intakes.

Snobeck won the second heat at the Nürburgring in May and another second heat at Brno in Czechoslovakia later that month. Cecotto won both heats at the Avus in late May, and both heats again at the Hungaroring in Budapest in August. There were strong finishes throughout the season by the Snobeck cars, but the best performer turned out to be Roland Asch. The DTM points system rewarded consistency, and Asch finished well up in many races, having worked out the best suspension set-up for his car. At the end of the 1988 season, he finished second overall, behind Klaus Ludwig in a Sierra and ahead of Hahne in another Ford.

1989: THE FIRST EVO

There were more format changes for the 1989 DTM season, which became more exciting through the addition of a single-lap shootout race at the start. The fastest twenty drivers in qualifying were eligible to compete in this, with four being eliminated and sixteen going through to the main heats. Places from seventeen onwards would then be determined by a qualifying race and there would once again be two heats. The 1989 cars also had to run with catalytic converters, in line with legislation in West Germany that now required all new cars to have one.

Mercedes attacked the new season with determination. Back at Stuttgart, they had created a new division called Sport-Technik to combine the racing activities associated with the DTM and with the Group C sports prototypes. Recognizing that the 2.3-16 cars were not going to be winners during 1988, they had also started looking at an improved car for 1989. It appears that they tested a turbocharged 2.3-16 before settling on a long-stroke 2.5-litre version of the 16-valve engine. This was announced in the roadgoing 190E 2.5-16 in autumn 1988, but it was only a first stage in creating the new 1989 DTM racer. That car would have a number of further improvements, which would be homologated through the limited-edition 190E 2.5-16 Evolution car (usually now known as the Evo 1) that was announced at Geneva in March 1989.

The late arrival of this car meant that the required 500 examples had not been built by the start of the DTM season, so the Mercedes teams came to the first few rounds with 2.3-litre cars. However, homologation was achieved in May and the new 2.5-litre cars made their first appearance that month.

From five works-supported teams in 1988, Mercedes had cut back to just three for the new season. These were AMG, Snobeck Racing Service and a newcomer, MS-Jet Racing. The latter fielded cars numbered 4 and 5 for Roland Asch and Manuel Reuter, respectively. The Snobeck works drivers were Dany Snobeck (in car 11) and Alain Cudini (12), while the AMG drivers were Kurt Thiim (2) and Klaus Ludwig (1). Ludwig was the previous year's DTM champion and had been tempted away from Ford by AMG. Mid-season, Jo Winkelhock would deputize for Ludwig in Round 7 at the Norsiring and Round 8 at Hockenheim when Ludwig was out of action after a medical operation.

Marko RSM were understandably disappointed not to be one of the teams selected for works support this year, but they nonetheless bravely entered the DTM. Their drivers were Jörg van Ommen (car 28) and Karl Wendlinger III (29); at mid-season, Roland Ratzenberger also entered the fray, with car number 59. Schwaben Motorsport had two cars: number 20 for Siegfried Müller Jr and number

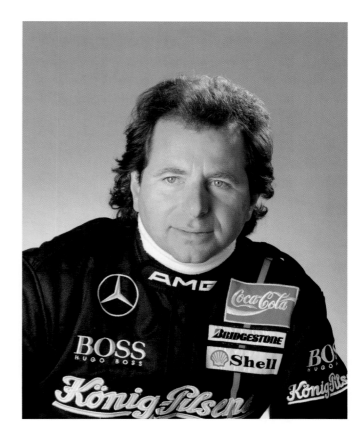

Klaus Ludwig was the lead driver in the works teams in the early 1990s, and would be the one who would win the championship title in 1992. This picture dates from 1991.

21 for Harald Becker. There were also Mercedes entries from BB Motorsport (Armin Bernhard in car number 60) and BMK Motorsport (Ralf-Werner Müller in car number 35). However, the privateers found the going hard this year, as the intense competition among the works teams raised standards and made the racing more and more expensive.

Until mid-season, Thiim in the AMG team and Reuter at MS-Jet were the leading Mercedes drivers. Each of the three works teams entered a single 2.5-litre car at the Mainz-Finthen round in mid-May, but without result. Neither Ludwig nor Snobeck finished; the best result was a ninth place for Asch in the second heat. At the Avus circuit a few weeks later the results were much more promising: Ludwig won the first heat, with Reuter in fourth place; Reuter also came third in the second heat. By the time of the sixth round, at the Nürburgring, all six Mercedes works drivers had the new cars.

Much to Mercedes' consternation, there was a seventh Evo car at the Nürburgring, put together by the Marko RSM team themselves with parts obtained through contacts in the Mercedes organization. Following a fairly bitter confrontation before the racing began, Jörg van Ommen was allowed to drive the Marko car at this meeting – with the proviso that it would be at this meeting only. In future, the Marko team would have to confine themselves to the 2.3-litre cars; no doubt the alternative would cause difficulties in their relationship with Mercedes. The best van Ommen could manage at the Nürburgring in his Evo was ninth place in the first heat.

The new Evo cars had been developed with Snobeck Racing Service, who did the suspension work and the new aluminium parts. They had a lightweight carbon-fibre boot lid that weighed just 1kg, and they pioneered 18-inch wheels in the DTM. The regulations stipulated that racing wheels could be no more than 2 inches larger than the wheels on the roadgoing car used for homologation, which is why the roadgoing Evo was made available with 16-inch wheels. The new wheels with their wider rims were accompanied by changes to the track and also to the wheelbase, all of which contributed to improved handling.

With 315PS at 8,500rpm and 285Nm of torque at 7,000rpm, the new cars returned some encouraging placings, but the teams had to develop them continually in order to remain competitive. It soon became apparent that Mercedes would have to go a step further in pursuit of their ultimate goal of winning the DTM. From August, work began at Stuttgart on another new car, which would become the legendary Evo II.

Despite the promise that the Evo I cars showed, the 1989 title fell to BMW driver Roberto Ravaglia. Ford had put up strong opposition but had faced multiple objections about the weight of their turbocharged cars and about the size of their air restrictors. For 1990, turbochargers would be banned from the DTM, so the company decided to cut its losses and quit the series at the end of 1989. The Mercedes works teams had to go home content with fourth place, which had gone to Kurt Thiim.

1990: ENTER THE EVO II

The fierce competition between Mercedes and BMW had helped to attract huge worldwide interest in the DTM.

Klaus Ludwig had been tempted over from Ford, and is pictured here driving the latest Evolution II racer in the Touring Car Grand Prix at Nürburgring, on 3 September 1990.

**Also pictured in the September 1990 Nürburgring race, this is Roland Asch
with an Evolution II, driving for Snobeck Racing Service.**

Although Ford had dropped out for the 1990 season, there was a new contender from Audi. Their 3.6-litre V8-engined car with four-wheel drive provoked immediate objections from the other teams, which persisted even after a weight penalty had been imposed on Audi. BMW raised their game, too, with the M3 Evolution. Opel also brought their new Omega to the series, although this was not initially competitive.

Mercedes again entered three works teams, but this time there were eight cars because the AMG team provided two cars for their junior drivers as well as the two for their primary drivers. These were Kurt Thiim in car number 6 and Klaus Ludwig in car number 7. The junior drivers changed around during the season. They started with Thomas Winkelhock in car 66 and Fritz Kreutzpointner in car 77, but Winkelhock was out of the team after an accident in Round 6 at Wunstorf. In his place came Karl Wendlinger III, formerly with the Marko team, who drove car number 60 from Round 8 in June. Briton Robb Gravett was given a drive in car 64 during Round 10 in September at the Nürburgring.

There was a second ex-Marko driver among the Mer-

cedes works drivers this year, as Jörg van Ommen had car number 17 for MS-Jet Racing. His partner was Frank Biela in car 16. The third works team was once again Snobeck Racing Service. Alain Cudini retained his position, this year in car 15, but Dany Snobeck stepped back to give car 14 to Roland Asch. Just one more Mercedes figured in the 1990 DTM, and that was car number 40, entered by privateer BAS Reifendienst (a tyre specialist from Deilingen) for Armin Bernhard. Initially, Bernhard had an older 2.3-litre car, but from May and the fourth round, at the Avus circuit, he was able to use a 2.5-litre Evo model.

The Mercedes teams contended the first rounds with Evo I cars, but the new Evo II with its huge wings was homologated on 1 May. It made its track debut in June at Round 7, held on the Nordschleife of the Nürburgring. Just two cars were available and they were given to AMG drivers Ludwig and Thiim. However, they did not yet offer the answer that Mercedes were looking for: despite leading the field in qualifying and leading the race, Ludwig was slowed by a fuel pump malfunction, and then both he and Thiim were put out of action by punctures.

The Evo II was soon rolled out to all the Mercedes works drivers. In the beginning, its engines made about 330PS at 8,500rpm, but later in the season power went as high as 360PS (thanks to the special F1 fuel that some teams used), with torque of 290Nm at 7,000rpm. With a racing weight of 1,040kg and wide tracks, the Evo II ran with a 110-litre fuel tank instead of a spare wheel to lower its centre of gravity. The driver's seat had also been moved back a little to improve the balance and once again there was no PAS.

The cars had ABS (a pioneering move) and a version of the latest Mercedes ASD replaced the earlier mechanical limited-slip differential. It was set permanently to give a 75 per cent lock-up. The cars started with 18-inch wheels that had 9-inch rims, but from Round 9 at Diepholz in August the wheel size was increased to 19 inches. Although Thiim finally won a heat, the revisions seemed to make no difference.

Sadly, Mercedes would go on to have a dreadful season,

with more than their share of bad luck and also problems with the handicap weights of both Evo I and Evo II cars. As the season neared its end, it looked very much as if Cecotto in the BMW M3 Evo would be the winner, but then Audi used team tactics to gain an advantage. By entering more cars for the last few rounds, they ended up winning, with the championship going to Hans Stuck.

The season finale was a non-championship DTM invitation race held at Kyalami in South Africa in November. Not all the drivers and teams attended – South Africa's apartheid policies persuaded some to stay away – but twenty-five cars did go. Among them were five AMG cars, and the drivers included Roland Asch, who took the test car with ABS. The event also offered new signing Ellen Lohr a first drive, although a damaged oil line put her car out of contention. Asch was finally declared the winner of the event, with Ludwig just three points behind him.

After the event: the car was driven by Roland Asch in the DTM invitation race at Kyalami in South Africa on 18 November 1990. He came second in the first heat and won the second.

1991: SO CLOSE FOR LUDWIG

Competition in the DTM was increasingly heated for the 1991 season, which became very exciting as a result. BMW were still fighting hard but their results tailed off a little after mid-season. Audi and Opel competed with Evolution versions of the V8 and the Omega, complete with splitters and wings to emulate those on the Mercedes Evo II. Opel still failed to make much impact, because the competition had moved on quite decisively. BMW and Mercedes made their case for adding more handicap weight to the Audis, but it was denied; Audi used tactics and teamwork to great advantage in the later stages of the season and went home with the championship. Their winning driver Frank Biela was probably delighted that he had switched his allegiance from Mercedes.

The ten rounds of the DTM included a new venue at Singen, which was a street race and quite different from the other nine track-based rounds. Although it was characterized by multiple incidents and accidents as the drivers came to terms with the different style of circuit, by all accounts they enjoyed the challenge. The DTM rounds were followed this year by two rounds of the ITR Cup, which did not count towards the drivers' title but did count towards the team and manufacturer rankings. Both were held in October, the first at Brno (Czechoslovakia) and the second at Donington in England. They were followed in December by a DTM Invitation race at Kyalami in South Africa. The ITR races had their own drivers' championship and, like the DTM title, this one went to Frank Biela from the Audi team.

Mercedes supported four works teams for 1991, with no fewer than ten cars; perhaps they were taking a leaf out of the Audi book of race tactics. AMG, MS-Jet Racing and Snobeck Racing Service were already well established but Zakspeed was new to the Mercedes fold after changing allegiance from BMW. They brought with them their lead driver, Fabien Giroix (car 18), who was teamed with Roland Asch (car 19). When Giroix proved inconsistent, he was replaced by Michael Schumacher in car 20 from the sixth round at the Norisring in June.

AMG's two senior drivers remained Kurt Thiim (car 7) and Klaus Ludwig (car 8), while Fritz Kreutzpointner remained in the junior team with car 87. He was joined by Ellen Lohr in car 78. Alain Cudini still led the two-car Snobeck team in car number 9, but his team-mate in car 10 this year was former Formula 1 star Jacques Laffite. The fourth Mercedes works team was MS-Jet Racing, who initially entered three

cars: Frank Schmickler had car 22, Jörg van Ommen car 23 and Jochen Mass car 24. Later in the season, from Round 8 at the Nürburgring in September, Mass's place in the team was taken by Bernd Schneider in car number 88. As for privateers, BAS Reifendienst clung on doggedly with their driver Armin Bernhard in car 50.

All the Mercedes works drivers had the latest versions of the Evo II, with a maximum weight of 980kg. Nine of the ten cars had ABS; BMW also used ABS this year, but the other teams had not yet developed their own racing systems. For Mercedes, it proved to be a mixed blessing, with two collisions on the rough-surfaced Avus circuit in May being attributed to the new system. In one of them, Kurt

Bernd Schneider first raced a 190 in the DTM for MS-Jet Racing in 1988 and later became a regular driver, winning four races against the five that earned Klaus Ludwig the championship in 1992. He is pictured here in 2007. ANGMOKIO/WIKIMEDIA COMMONS

Michael Schumacher, later Formula 1 World Champion, and Karl Wendlinger both drove in some DTM rounds. They are pictured here in 1991 during their time with the Sauber-Mercedes Group C sports-racing team.

Thiim rammed the BMW of Johnny Cecotto; in the second, Ellen Lohr rammed Thiim's car. Power in the 1991 Evo II was claimed to be 340PS at 8,800rpm, a little down on the best figures from the 1990 season, and torque was posted at 300Nm at 7,000rpm. Some of the cars had six-speed gearboxes while others had the familiar five-speed type. Some cars had 18-inch wheels and others had the 19-inch size that had been introduced towards the end of the 1990 season.

The Mercedes cars were very competitive this year, but they seemed to be dogged by bad luck, and results were rather patchy. The first two rounds were disappointing, although Klaus Ludwig found his form in April during the third round at the Nürburgring, when he won the first heat. Ellen Lohr consistently demonstrated fast qualifying times and won the qualifying race at the Avus circuit in May. Round 6 at the Norisring in June brought more success, with Kurt Thiim winning the first heat and coming second in the second one, while Roland Asch finished third in both of them. There was then a Mercedes spectacular at the Nürburgring in September, when the works cars took the top four places in the first heat and the top three in the second. It was nevertheless not quite enough; Klaus Ludwig had to be satisfied with second place in the drivers' championship behind

Biela, while the next best-placed Mercedes driver was Alain Cudini, who finished sixth.

Despite the best efforts of his team-mates, Ludwig was unable to win the drivers' title in the two ITR races either, and in the Kyalami invitation event he finished third behind Kurt Thiim. The winner was Johnny Cecotto in a BMW Sport Evolution. Perhaps it was these near-misses that spurred him on to higher things in 1992.

The Kyalami event was of course intended to bring the thrills and spills of the DTM to a wider audience and, as in 1990, did not count towards any championship points. Not all the regular drivers were present, although it is worth recording that at least two teams provided Evo IIs for guest drivers. MS-Jet Racing provided car number 20 for local driver Chris Aberdein, who did rather well in it. BAS Reifendienst meanwhile provided two cars, one numbered 35 for regular driver Armin Bernhard and another numbered 34 for Helge Probst. Lastly, Michael Hess took the wheel of car number 13, which is not attributed to any of the DTM teams in surviving records.

1992: VICTORY AT LAST

The 1992 DTM was scheduled to be the last one run to Group A rules and with the existing weight handicapping system. Although the 1992 regulations were still essentially those of Group A, competitors were allowed a little more freedom with engines.

Audi took the extra freedom too far, and quit in a huff mid-season when their 180-degree crankshaft was declared illegal. Opel did not compete this year, having realized that the Omega was never going to be a winner; instead, they focused their efforts on preparing the Calibra coupé for the new Class 1 of the 1993 championship. So it was left to Mercedes and BMW to slug it out through the twelve championship rounds. That made the racing even more exciting, as neither side had any intention of going home without the prize and the two teams were very evenly matched. Sometime it was just their choice of tyre that made the decisive difference.

Mercedes were back to just three works teams this year, who entered eight cars. Having battled heroically in the DTM ever since 1985, Snobeck Racing Service chose this year to focus their efforts on running a pair of Evo II models in the French Super Tourisme Championship. That left AMG, MS-Jet Racing and Zakspeed in the DTM, along with

Four of the 1992 works cars and all eight drivers line up for a publicity picture: (left to right) Jacques Laffite, Jörg van Ommen, Bernd Schneider, Klaus Ludwig, Kurt Thiim, Roland Asch, Ellen Lohr and Keke Rosberg.

two privateers who ran Mercedes. One was BAS Reifendienst, whose regular driver Armin Bernhard this year drove car number 27. The other was Manthey Racing, with car 55 for Olaf Manthey, which put in its first appearance in mid-season at the Nordschleife race, in Round 6 of the series.

There had been some shuffling of drivers between one team and another, although most of the names were familiar.

Fielding four cars, AMG's senior drivers were Klaus Ludwig (car 3) and Bernd Schneider (car 4). The juniors were Ellen Lohr in car 5 and Keke Rosberg in car 6; Rosberg could hardly be considered a 'junior' as he was a former Formula One world champion, but he was certainly new to the team. The two cars from MS-Jet Racing were number 11 for Jacques Laffite and number 12 for Jörg van Ommen, and the

Pictured together at the Touring Car Grand Prix held at the Nürburgring on 20 September 1992 are Mercedes drivers Bernd Schneider, Klaus Ludwig and Kurt Thiim.

ABOVE: **Kurt Thiim,
driving for the Zakspeed
team, was victorious at
the first DTM race of
the 1992 season. This
was the Bergischer
Löwe, held at Zolder in
Belgium on 5 April.**

**The DTM round at
Diepholz Airfield on
16 August 1992 was
a complete triumph
for Klaus Ludwig, who
won both heats. He
is pictured crossing
the finishing line in his
Evolution II racer.**

Zakspeed drivers were Roland Asch (car 17) and Kurt Thiim (car 18). All of these were experienced people; Mercedes was taking no chances in the final DTM season before the rules changed.

A third driver would join the Zakspeed cohort mid-season, when someone called 'John Winter' entered for the team at the Diepholz round in August with car number 28. 'John Winter' was really Louis Krages, a German businessman who had always raced under a pseudonym to prevent his family from finding out about his hobby. Inevitably, his true identity had been revealed when he was part of the winning Porsche crew at the Le Mans 24 Hours event in 1985, but he continued to use the pseudonym, which had become well established.

The 1992 Evo II racers had moved on once again. Both power-assisted steering and servo-assisted brakes were in the specification, and the cars were still able to meet the 980kg weight requirement thanks to extensive use of car-bon fibre. (The peculiarities of the DTM handicap system meant that privateers using those same cars had to meet a weight limit of just 950kg.) The cars ran on 19-inch wheels. New for 1992 was an XTrac six-speed clutchless transmission. The engines, meanwhile, were claimed to deliver 373PS at 9,500rpm and 300Nm of torque at 7,750rpm. Crankshaft speeds of up to 10,200rpm have been claimed for these late engines, so it was no surprise that each one needed a major rebuild every few hundred kilometres.

For once, most things went right for Mercedes. The BMW Schnitzer team had a really bad season with the M3. The best-placed BMW driver was Johnny Cecotto, around whom a new Fina racing team had been built; he finished fourth in the championship. Despite a spate of driveshaft troubles at the Norisring in June, which was Round 7 of the series, the Mercedes drivers returned some solid results. Ellen Lohr in particular was delighted to win both heats at Hockenheim during May, making her the first female driver

Ellen Lohr won the first heat at the Hockenheim Motorsport Festival on 24 May 1992, and is seen being congratulated by team-mate Klaus Ludwig. She was the first woman ever in the history of the DTM to win a race, and also posted the fastest lap of 1:05:35 min in her AMG-Mercedes Evolution II.

ABOVE: **At the 24-hour DTM race held on the Nordschleife of the Nürburgring on 18 June 1992, Klaus Ludwig won both of the day's races.**

Mercedes still proudly owns Klaus Ludwig's 1992 DTM-winning Evolution II racer.

Rebuilt by Mercedes-Benz Classic for use in historic motorsport events, this Evolution II
is pictured at the Mercedes-Benz Classic Insight '125 Years of Motorsports' in April 2019
at Silverstone, together with Mercedes-Benz brand ambassador Klaus Ludwig.

ever to win a DTM round. Mercedes drivers won sixteen of the twenty-four races this season, with five going to Klaus Ludwig and four to Bernd Schneider.

So it was that Mercedes achieved the victory that they had been striving for since the start of the DTM in 1986. Klaus Ludwig carried off the title and his success was underpinned by Kurt Thiim in second place, by Keke Rosberg in fifth, by Roland Asch in sixth and by Jörg van Ommen in tenth. AMG took home the team title. The Evo II had finally dominated the DTM series and given Mercedes the manufacturers' title.

1993: A BRIEF AFTERLIFE

At the end of the 1992 season, BMW decided to join Audi and Opel in stepping away from the DTM series, although inevitably their absence would not be permanent. For a time,

Mercedes debated whether to compete under the new rules as well, and it seemed that Alfa Romeo might be the only factory team in the series.

Mercedes' problem was partly caused by the fact that they were due to replace the W201 compact saloons with the new W202 C Class cars in summer 1993. There was no time to develop a W202 car for the new series, but they clearly felt that it would be a mistake not to participate. They decided, therefore, to mount a holding operation by entering with the 1992 Evo II cars modified to the new Class 1 specification. This was not dissimilar to the old Group A, but it was limited to cars with an engine size of 2.5 litres and with no more than six cylinders – a formula that rather pointedly excluded the Audi V8s. It was also far more liberal, permitting cars to be constructed from carbon fibre and to feature electronic driver aids. The new DTM would also have a Class 2, but the 1993 series attracted very few entries.

Nevertheless, a full complement of Evo II cars lined up at Zolder for the first round of the 1993 series in early April. Most had the 1992 specification, somewhat modified to suit the new regulations, but a crash development programme had delivered the first examples of a 1993-specification car for drivers Klaus Ludwig and Bernd Schneider. By the time of the second round at Hockenheim later that month, there was a third car with the new specification, and the 1993 cars were gradually rolled out to all the works teams. Not a lot was different from the 1992 cars,

but the use of a dry sump did allow the new cars to be lower to the ground.

The factory-supported teams came from AMG and Zakspeed, with a third one branded as the DTM Junior Team. AMG had four cars: number 1 for Klaus Ludwig, number 2 for Ellen Lohr, number 11 for Bernd Schneider and number 12 for Roland Asch. Ludwig's car was the only one to have the 1993 specification from the start, and was the only one at the first round in Zolder. Schneider joined in with a second 1993-spec car at Round 2, and the others followed. In

ABOVE: **Keeping the Mercedes flag flying during the 1993 DTM season were (left to right) drivers Roland Asch, Bernd Schneider, Ellen Lohr, Klaus Ludwig, Kurt Thiim and Jörg van Ommen.**

At the Eifelrennen race on the Nürburgring on 2 May 1993, Kurt Thiim leads the pack in a Class 1 version of the W201. Right behind is one of the Alfa Romeos that dominated the season.

The racing liveries of different teams always excite interest. This accurate drawing by Oliver Pohlmann shows the livery of Armin Berhard's 1993 DTM racer. OLIVER POHLMANN/WIKIMEDIA COMMONS

The Mercedes-Benz Classic Evolution II, pictured on 30 March 2017 in the paddock at a track day held at Hockenheim...

... and on the track at the same event. Instead of sponsors' decals, the car now carries an advertisement for the Mercedes All Time Stars classic sales department.

Roland Asch with a 1992 DTM car at the 2017 Nürburgring Classics event. The Evolution II cars are always a draw at historic motorsport events.

early rounds, Asch and Lohr used 1992-spec cars, and their 1993 cars did not become available until Round 5 at the Nordschleife. Ludwig, complaining of vibration in his 1993 car, switched to a 1992 vehicle for the second heat at Round 3.

Zakspeed initially entered two cars: number 3 for Kurt Thiim and number 4 for Jörg van Ommen. Thiim had a 1993-spec car from Round 2, his first appearance in this series, but van Ommen had to make do with a 1992 car until Round 5 at the Nordschleife. Car 3 was then given to new driver Giorgio Francia right at the end of the series for Round 10 at Hockenheim in September. The new DTM Junior Team in effect took over from the junior section of the AMG team as a training ground for new drivers; for 1993, they had Alexander 'Sandy' Gray in car 20 and Stig Amthor in car 23. While Gray was recovering from an injury, Heinz-Harald Frentzen replaced him for Round 10 at Hockenheim. Frentzen was due to drive car number 46 but was not allowed to start because he had left his racing licence behind in Japan, where he had been racing in Formula Nippon events.

The privateer teams that entered Mercedes this year were different again. MS-Jet Racing had been dissolved and its remains had been absorbed into a new team called Persson. The BAS Reifendienst team, now rebranded as BAS Reifen-technik, clung doggedly on. Persson had a pair of Evo IIs: number 16 for Uwe Alzen and number 17 for Olaf Manthey. From Round 8 at Singen they fielded a third car, numbered 44 and driven by Markus Oestrich. BAS Reifentechnik were late to the party, their first entry being at Round 4 in Wunstorf with car number 38 driven by Ralf Kludt. At Round 5, held on the Nordschleife of the Nürburgring, car 39 joined in, with Axel Göbel at the wheel. Not until Round 8 at Singen did regular driver Armin Bernhard make an appearance. The delays, presumably, were caused by modifying the cars to meet the new Class 1 standards.

The Mercedes cars and their drivers put up a good fight throughout the 1993 series, but this year's DTM was dominated by the four Alfa Romeo entries, with V6 engines and four-wheel drive. Victory went to Nicola Larini, who won the championship again in 1994. By that time, Mercedes had developed its new C Class racer, and AMG drivers Roland Asch and Bernd Schneider demonstrated its potential by finishing in third and fourth place, respectively. A few older Evo IIs to Class 1 specification remained in use, by the DTM Junior Team and Persson Motorsport, but it was clear that the W201-based cars had reached the end of their days in top-line motorsport.

The same car pictured at the Classic Insight '125 Years of Motorsports' event at Silverstone, April 2019.

CHAPTER EIGHT

CUSTOMIZED AND TUNED

The Mercedes 190 range was born into a period when the fashion for customizing and performance tuning expensive cars had reached new heights in Germany. There had of course been an aftermarket tuning industry for many years. Its leading name had always been AMG, who had been working on Mercedes models since 1967. They worked mostly on individual commissions in the early days, many of which were for competition use and were very rare. By the 1980s, several other aftermarket enhancement specialists had joined in, offering cosmetic modifications as well as performance upgrades.

Among the newcomers were a number of firms who were prepared to create hugely expensive bespoke coachwork. These had grown up to meet a demand for highly individualized cars from the Middle East, where levels of wealth for some had risen significantly after the oil price rises in 1974,

and where it was more or less a social obligation for individuals to advertise that wealth. The newly rich were developing a taste for Western luxury goods, and of course that included expensive cars. It had become commonplace for owners to try to outdo one another by ordering cars with more and more individual features. The Germans adopted the English word 'tuner' into their own language as Tuner, to describe all these aftermarket conversion specialists, even though some of them focused only on cosmetic work and not on the performance upgrades that the word suggests.

When the W201 came along, it was immediately snapped up as another model that the Tuner specialists could work on. By 1984, if not earlier, the first conversions were available, and these and their successors remained on sale in Germany into the 1990s, even though the custom for extravagantly modified vehicles had abated somewhat in the Middle East.

It is worth noting that Mercedes-Benz did not give their approval for any of these conversions (except, latterly, those by AMG). Although they tended to look the other way because a thriving aftermarket was good for business, they occasionally insisted that the converters should remove all Mercedes badges from the cars they completed.

There were many more conversions and enhancements than this chapter is able to cover. The following is intended to give a flavour of what was available.

One early customer for the AMG 2.3-litre W201 was ex-Beatle Ringo Starr. His 1984 car is seen on display at the Mercedes-Benz Museum in Stuttgart in June 2013. VALDER137/WIKIMEDIA COMMONS

AMG

Hans-Werner Aufrecht and Erhard Melcher founded AMG in 1967 to

Probably no two examples of the **AMG** car were exactly the same; simply having right-hand drive made this one a rarity. The badges, painted in the body colour, read **190E** on the left and **AMG** on the right. VALDER137/ WIKIMEDIA COMMONS

develop and sell high-performance Mercedes models. The A and the M came from their surnames, and the G was for Grossaspach, Aufrecht's birthplace and the site of their first premises. Both men had once worked for Mercedes in Stuttgart and their new business remained geographically close to the factory. Expansion later prompted a move to new headquarters at nearby Affalterbach.

Initially independent, AMG gradually became closer to

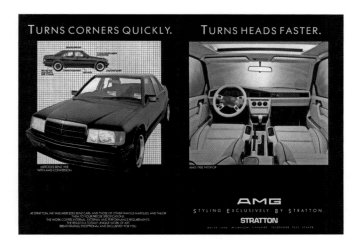

TURNS CORNERS QUICKLY. TURNS HEADS FASTER.

AMG
STYLING EXCLUSIVELY BY STRATTON.
STRATTON

The Stratton dealership in London handled AMG products in Britain. This was their sales brochure for the 2.3-litre car. MAGIC CAR PICS

Mercedes, and from the mid-1980s ran one of the works teams using W201s in the DTM (see Chapter 7). During 1990, they were absorbed into Mercedes, becoming the company's equivalent of BMW's famed Motorsport division.

The earliest AMG model based on the W201 became available in 1984 and was known as the AMG 190E 2.3. As that name suggests, it had a 2.3-litre engine, but of course this was at a time when the largest engine available in Europe was the 122PS 2.0-litre in the 190E. AMG bored out the 2.0-litre block themselves to achieve the 2.3-litre capacity and, with other modifications typical of the brand, they achieved a power output of 160PS at 5,750rpm and torque of 215Nm at 4,750rpm. Their car accelerated to 100km/h from rest in 8.6 seconds, and would go on to a top speed of 216km/h (134mph).

These performance figures were of course eclipsed by the factory's own 190E 2.3-16 that arrived a few months later, but the AMG car was hot property in the first months of 1984. It also set the tone for later AMG developments of the W201, with gently flared front wings covering wide wheels and tyres, sports front seats, additional wood trim and a leather-rimmed steering wheel. A bodykit of front aprons, sills and rear spoiler was available and it is probable that no two AMG 190E 2.3 cars were exactly alike because customers could choose their specification from a menu of options. However, one thing that seems to have been common to

AMG also turned their hands to bespoke interiors like this one, which had sports seats, a branded steering wheel, and additional wood trim on the dashboard. AMG

An early publicity picture for the AMG car, showing it with only an AMG badge on the boot lid. The car was described as an AMG 230E, which probably did not please Mercedes, who had their own 230E as a variant of the W124 range. AMG

Publicity picture showing the boot spoiler's semi-circular cut-out, designed to clear the three-pointed star badge. The wheels have clearly been added to the picture with an airbrush, but are of a style that did become available. AMG

all the conversions was that AMG painted all the chrome on the car in the body colour, including the badges. It was a feature that would be used on later AMG W201s as well.

The next major AMG model based on the W201 was introduced in 1988 as the 190E 3.2 AMG. This was based on the six-cylinder 190E 2.6, with its engine bored out to 90mm to give 3205cc; new pistons raised the compression ratio to 10:1 and a new camshaft helped to increase power to 248PS (245bhp) with torque of 318Nm (234lb ft). Allied to a 3.27:1 rear axle ratio, this gave a claimed maximum speed of 152mph (245km/h). The five-speed manual car reached 60mph in 6.2 seconds, and with the four-speed automatic option the 0–60mph dash took exactly 7 seconds.

The suspension was lowered and stiffened and the car ran on 16-inch cast alloy wheels with 7.5-inch rims and 245/45 VR 16 tyres. The wheels could be had in a five-spoke design or in the smooth-faced 'aero' style, and there were ventilated front brake discs as standard. Inevitably, there was a bodykit of spoilers and sills, and the trademark AMG all-over paint finish was standard. Options on the interior menu included special steering wheels, Recaro sports seats, wood trim kits, special shift grips, branded floor mats, and so on.

AMG models became available through Mercedes showrooms after the tuning company had joined forces with the manufacturer in October 1990. However, these were somewhat tamed to resemble the standard products more closely. By 1992 there was an AMG 190E 2.6, and the original AMG 190E 3.2 was re-specified from February that year to use an AMG-tuned version of the four-valve 3.2-litre engine that had been introduced in the 300SE models during 1991. This latter engine had 233PS at 5,750rpm and, with an automatic gearbox, gave a maximum speed of 244km/h (152mph) and could reach 100km/h from rest in 7.7 seconds. The 3.2-litre car was available in only six colours

A 1992 AMG 190E 2.6 for the UK market. After
AMG became part of Mercedes in 1990, the
AMG offerings were toned down a little. AMG

A new model from AMG late in the W201's life
had a tuned version of the 3.2-litre four-valve
engine seen in Mercedes' larger models. AMG

AMG 190E 3.2: the all-one-colour finish was
characteristic of AMG and the brand's letters
were moulded into the GRP tail spoiler.

from the standard 201 range: Almandine Red, Arctic White,
Black, Blue-Black metallic, Brilliant Silver and Bornite.

BRABUS

German Tuner Brabus was established in 1977, the name
coming from the surnames of its founder Bodo Buschmann
and of the friend with whom he established the company,
Klaus Brackman. German law required two people to establish a company, but Brackman had no intention of becoming
further involved and sold his shares to Buschmann almost
immediately.

This early 190E from
Brabus was very much in
the traditional German
Tuner mould, with a
focus on performance
rather than cosmetics.
The painted mirror
bodies, blacked-out
grille and lattice-
spoke alloy wheels
were nevertheless
distinguishing touches.
BRABUS

The company's primary focus was always on performance through engine tuning, but it also offered cosmetic modifications such as bodykits and multi-piece alloy wheels. Generally speaking, a Brabus 190E was relatively discreet to look at – at least by comparison with some of the efforts from rival tuners.

CARAT DUCHATELET

Duchatelet was a Belgian company based in Liège that had specialized in armour-plating cars before the 1980s. It did not offer engine enhancements for the W201 and even its lowered suspension package was really focused on appearance, often being matched by attractive alloy wheels and wide tyres.

The company marketed its Mercedes enhancements under the Carat brand, describing them in the sales literature as 'Carat by Duchatelet'. There was a bodykit of spoilers and side skirts, and the front apron incorporated cutouts for additional auxiliary lighting. The main focus of the Duchatelet work was on the interior, with retrims, wood trim kits and special steering wheels.

Duchatelet were more concerned with appearance enhancements than with performance. This car from their Carat range clearly demonstrates their approach. DUCHATELET

A rear view of the same car shows the Carat Duchatelet badge and the squared-off tops to the wheel-arch extensions, which gave the car a more purposeful air. DUCHATELET

Another Carat Duchatelet creation, this time deliberately sleek and sharp rather than low and menacing. DUCHATELET

Later models had this badge on the boot lid. The paint colour was also a custom finish applied by Duchatelet.

High-quality interior retrims were another Duchatelet speciality. DUCHATELET

The white steering wheel carries the Carat Duchatelet name and the white instrument faces contrast strongly with their black background panel. DUCHATELET

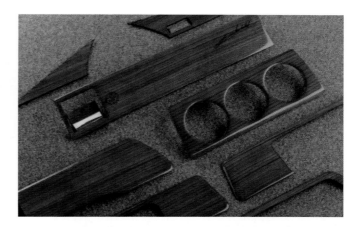

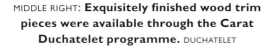

MIDDLE RIGHT: Exquisitely finished wood trim pieces were available through the Carat Duchatelet programme. DUCHATELET

BOTTOM RIGHT: Even the cover of the sales brochure embodied the essence of the Duchatelet approach.

JANSPEED

In Britain, turbocharging specialist Janspeed of Salisbury in Wiltshire had a conversion for the 190E ready by 1985. It was, read the sales leaflet, 'a car for the discerning enthusiast who wants the refinement of the compact Mercedes yet requires the benefits of enhanced performance and more individuality in exterior styling'.

The heart of the conversion was a single RotoMaster RM60 turbocharger delivering 6psi, drawing its air through an intercooler. The engine retained its standard 9.1:1 compression but there was an additional electronic control unit to alter the ignition timing and advance as needed, and to provide protection against over-boost and over-revving. Janspeed also fitted a high-flow stainless steel exhaust system with low back pressure.

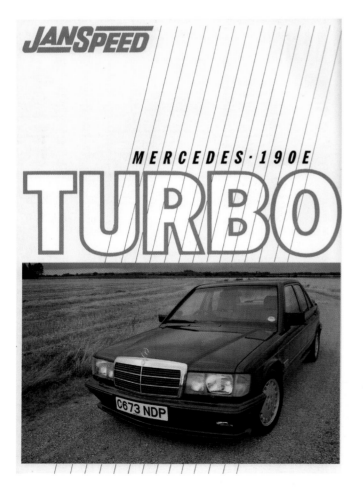

Janspeed turned out an extremely rapid 190E with the addition of subtle good looks provided by Lorinser.

The additional plumbing for the RotoMaster turbocharger is visible under the bonnet of a Janspeed modified car. JANSPEED

The only sign of the Janspeed conversion inside the car was a turbo boost gauge mounted on the dashboard. JANSPEED

With 179bhp (181PS) at 5,000rpm and torque peaking at 192lb ft (260Nm) at 4,000rpm, the turbocharged 190E was claimed to reach 141mph (227km/h). As agents for Lorinser, Janspeed suggested fitting that company's bodykit, with a leather-rimmed steering wheel and additional interior wood trim. The suggested wheels were 15-inch Mercedes alloys with 6.5-inch rims and wide 205/50 x 15 tyres.

LORINSER

Lorinser had started life in 1935 as a Mercedes dealership

at Winnenden near Stuttgart. The son of founder Erwin Lorinser became its managing director in 1974, and in 1976 created a subsidiary that would be dedicated specifically to aftermarket work with the standard factory products. By 1981, this subsidiary had become Sportservice Lorinser GmbH, with new headquarters at Waiblingen. Its focus was on performance modifications and cosmetic alterations for Mercedes-Benz models.

Among the Lorinser options for the W201 was a restyled front spoiler with cut-outs to take additional driving lights. For the 190E 2.3-16, the company had a second style that incorporated cut-outs for two auxiliary lights on each side. All these items were superbly finished. Lorinser also had its own 15-inch alloy wheels with 6.5-inch rims and a different offset from the standard Mercedes type, although the two wheels were very similar in appearance.

Lorinser developed some attractive and well-made body addenda for the W201, and added them to this early demonstrator. LORINSER

There was even a bodykit for the 16-valve car. This example demonstrates Lorinser's liking for decals – at least on its demonstrator models. LORINSER

MOSSELMAN

Dutch specialist Mosselman Turbo Systems had developed a turbocharger kit for the 190E by 1985, and subsequently also made one available to suit the 190E 2.3-16, which was supplied with a different inlet manifold to suit the 16-valve engine. The major components were a KKK turbocharger working at 5.5psi boost, an intercooler, a big-bore stainless steel exhaust and a Bosch fuel enrichment regulator. In a standard 190E, this combination raised power to around 190bhp (192PS) and gave a 0–60mph time of just over 7 seconds.

In Britain, the Mercedes-Benz main dealer in Eastleigh, David J Sparshatt, began offering a full performance conversion using the Mosselman kit during 1985. Sparshatt's complemented the engine conversion by lowered suspension that used Sachs Sporting components, with 225/50VR 15 tyres on Rial alloy wheels. They also added a Lorinser bodykit to help the car look the part of a high-performance model.

OETTINGER

Tuning company Oettinger is better known for its work with Volkswagen Group products than with Mercedes, but in 1985 it introduced a performance conversion for the 190E 2.3-16. The engine capacity was increased to 2593cc and

ABOVE: **The engine top cover makes clear that Oettinger had enlarged the capacity from 2.3 litres to 2.6 litres.**
OETTINGER

Only the name decal on the door indicates that this 16-valve car is not an ordinary 190E 2.3-16.
OETTINGER

the resulting car was known as an Oettinger 190E 2.6-16. The engine had 211PS at 5,700rpm and 286Nm (211lb ft) of torque at 4,300rpm. The car was claimed to accelerate from 0–100km/h in 7.4 seconds.

The last of these Oettinger conversions was probably built in 1988, when the new 'factory' 190E 2.5-16 was introduced. However, in 1990 Oettinger also built a single long-stroke conversion of a 190E 2.3-16, with a swept volume stretched to 2.8 litres. There was supposedly only one of these conversions, which unsurprisingly was known as an Oettinger 190E 2.8-16. Its engine is claimed to have delivered 288bhp (292PS) and to have given a top speed of 266km/h (165mph) with 0–100km/h acceleration of 5.5 seconds.

SCHULZ TUNING

Former Porsche design engineer Eberhard Schulz established Schulz Tuning at Korschenbroich near Neuss in Germany. His first major product was the Isdera Imperator supercar, which he put on sale in 1984. He had developed it from the CW311 show car, which had been designed by Schulz himself for Mercedes but had not been put into production by the Stuttgart company.

Schulz embraced the tuning and conversions business as well, and created some quite remarkable transformations. Some were so radical that they incurred the wrath of Mercedes-Benz, who took legal action to forbid the Schulz company from retaining the three-pointed star on some of the vehicles it converted. As a result, many of the sales brochure and publicity pictures have the star on the grille and tail somewhat crudely blacked out.

On the W201, the best-known Schulz creation was a two-door cabriolet based on a 190E, which cost around DM 100,000 at a time when the standard saloon cost around DM30,000. Schulz also offered the car with the 3.8-litre V8 engine from the contemporary Mercedes 380SE; in that case, the price rose to DM120,000. At least one car was built with this engine, but it is not clear how many cabriolets were built in all.

Schulz also developed a coupé version, adapting the lines of the 124-series coupés to suit the smaller car. MAGIC CAR PICS

Schulz produced some quite radical conversions of the W201, including this hugely attractive V8-engined two-door cabriolet.

The Schulz City hatchback conversion, pictured for publicity purposes next to a Volkswagen Golf of the same size. SCHULZ TUNING

Although of poor quality, this image shows that the tailgate has come from a 124-seres estate car! SCHULZ TUNING

Schulz also built some two-door coupés from the W201, basing their overall profile on that of the larger 124-series coupés. There were supposedly twenty-eight of these. Even more radical was what the company called the 190E 2.6 City, which was a shortened six-cylinder 190E with a hatchback. The first of these was built in 1990, and Schulz offered the conversion with either three or five doors, in both cases with the tail lights and tailgate from Mercedes' own 124-series estates. Not many of these conversions were built and the last was allegedly done in 1991.

SGS (STYLING-GARAGE)

Peter Engel and Chris Hahn founded Styling-Garage as a repair shop in the north German town of Pinneberg, near Hamburg. However, Engel soon left the business and from 1981 Hahn steered it in a different direction, to capitalize on the latest fashion for heavily modified cars. Also known as SGS, the company soon gained a reputation for the radical nature of its work. Despite upsetting Mercedes enough to be forbidden to use the three-pointed star on its conversions, Styling-Garage was very successful and produced some spectacular conversions for Middle Eastern customers before running into financial difficulties and folding in 1986.

On the W201, the company developed a typically radical model that it called the

Although the picture is actually an airbrush creation to illustrate the concept, SGS really did build this City Fun car. Note the SGS emblem on the modified grille, designed to resemble that on the big Mercedes SEC coupés. STYLING-GARAGE

The removable rear top panel was clear in the airbrushed concept picture. STYLING-GARAGE

BELOW: **Styling-Garage also created two examples of this four-door St Tropez cabriolet. This one was pictured in a special display at the 2017 Frankfurt Motor Show.**
MATTI BLUME/WIKIMEDIA COMMONS

City Fun. This had a shortened wheelbase and an adaptable body that could be transformed from open cabriolet to pick-up or estate car by adding or removing body sections. It is not clear how many of these were built, but at least one was made from what appears to have been a US-specification 190E 2.3.

There was also a four-door cabriolet, with full-height doors and a bracing bar across the roof space; two of these are claimed to have been built.

ZENDER

The German Zender company produced a very wide range of add-ons for many popular cars in the 1980s, and among them was of course the Mercedes W201. The company offered its own design of front apron, both with and without cut-outs to take additional driving lights. There were also alternative styles of boot-lid spoiler, various sill and flank panels, and several alloy wheel options.

Zender specialized in bolt-on body addenda, but also offered several styles of alloy wheel for the W201. ZENDER

A boot-lid spoiler, styled sill panels and alloy wheels gave this Zender-modified car its distinctive looks. ZENDER

BELOW: This Zender spoiler was quite neat, although the lower apron and heavy sills were perhaps less successful visually. ZENDER

ABOVE: The neat spoiler and five-spoke alloy wheels enabled this 190E 2.3 to stand out from the crowd. ZENDER

An alternative style of lower body cladding, a different front apron and a body-colour grille showed a different aspect of the Zender range. ZENDER

CHAPTER NINE

BUYING AND OWNING A MERCEDES W201

Older Mercedes cars tend to have a different kind of following from many other classics, perhaps because ownership is often as much to do with rational considerations as emotions. At the time when the 190s were available new, Mercedes had a reputation for building logical, rational cars that for the most part lacked the emotional appeal of, say, an Alfa Romeo or an MG. And the 190 really is a logical, rational and (mostly) unemotional car. It also makes for a solid, dependable and relatively inexpensive classic that you can actually use on a regular basis.

There are exceptions to this rule of thumb, of course. The Cosworth cars, and especially the Evolution models, do make a strong appeal to the heart as well as the head. When these cars were introduced, Mercedes was cautiously exploring what was really a new area of the market for the company, and later models benefited from their findings. But there is little doubt that the W201s as a whole belong to a distinct era in Mercedes history when nothing but the best would do. Nothing got past the corporate committees unless it had been very carefully thought through. The W201

A well-sorted 190 is a pleasure to drive. Cars such as this early UK-market 190E were a revelation when they were new, although nearly four decades later they may feel old and stodgy in comparison with their modern equivalents.

sold strongly, so it is not a rare car (except, of course, for the Evolution models), and its legendary durability means that a good proportion of the 1.8 million or so built have survived to this day.

CHOICE AND AVAILABILITY

Different models of the W201 range were available in different countries, but by far the most popular model globally was the 2.0-litre 190E. Outside the USA (where the equivalent model was the 190E 2.3), there will be plenty of these for sale. Similarly, there are good numbers of 190E 1.8s still around in Britain, where the car was popular, partly because

it was carefully priced within the mainstream company car bracket of its time. The 190E 2.6, by contrast, was much less common because of its high cost, although it did secure a worthwhile following. The 16-valve Cosworth cars were not especially numerous in right-hand-drive form, and the two Evolution models were only built with left-hand drive.

Diesel variants are more likely to be found on the European continent than in Britain, and will therefore have left-hand drive. A few stalwarts in Britain did buy the 190D or 190D 2.5, which were the only diesels available in that market, but diesel cars were still a minority interest there when the W201s were around. Their relatively poor performance also meant that few enthusiasts attempted to keep them going in later years.

Not a good starting point! The W201 is still in fairly plentiful supply, and a car like this – pictured in a scrapyard in Canada – is best considered as a source of spares only. FLICKR ©DAVE_7 FROM CANADA

The W201 has now passed through its 'cheap banger' stage, when cars like this 1991 190E 1.8 were de-badged and given a spoiler and AMG wheels to make them appear more glamorous. CHARLIE, CC 2.0/ WIKIMEDIA COMMONS

There are plenty of 190s around that have been modified and well maintained, such as this attractive 1985 example. As a prospective owner, however, you might prefer one in original condition. THINES J SHANKAR/WIKIMEDIA COMMONS

Your choice of a W201 may be influenced by availability as much as anything else. However, do remember that there is a greater depth to the range than most people realize. You may prefer the purity of the early models, or you may like the extra protective panels on the facelifted cars. You may insist on a manual gearbox; you may hanker after the superb motorway performance of a 190E 2.6; or you may want the exclusivity of a Cosworth. One way or another, there are a number of issues you should look out for when viewing a car that is for sale.

STRUCTURAL PROBLEMS

The W201s were built at a time when Mercedes build quality was legendary. The old cliché that the cars felt as if they were hewn from solid steel billet is worth remembering: the doors shut with a satisfying clunk and the whole car just feels hugely dependable.

The cars were so well made that any uneven panel gaps should be taken as a sign of trouble. The chances are that they will be the result of poorly repaired accident damage, and that should motivate you to check for any associated problems. However, accident damage is certainly not the only issue that can threaten the integrity of the W201's structure, and even though the cars were well protected when new, with galvanized elements and good-quality underseal, rust can get a hold in certain areas.

Small areas of rust in the front wings around the wheel arches should be immediately obvious. If the car has been fitted with chrome arch embellishers (and many were), have a good look to check that these embellishers are not hiding rust and that their fixings are not in fact the cause of it. Look at the base of the rear window, because rust can often start here, too.

Some other readily accessible areas may show rust. Have a look around the base of the radio aerial in the rear wing, around the edges of the rear light units, and even around the bolts that attach the rear number plate to the body. Check the rubber seal around the boot lock, too.

You can get a good idea of the overall condition of a W201's structure by examining the jacking points, which are behind covers in the sills. Rust here invariably means that there is rust elsewhere. In this case, you need to make a sensible appraisal of where it is and how serious it is. However, do not assume that no rust around the jacking points automatically means there will be no rust in the rest of the car!

It is worth checking for rust in some of the less visible areas of the car, too. Take a good look at the inner wings, both front and rear. Get underneath to make sure that the brake pipes – and pipes for optional hydraulic systems such as the SLS (self-levelling suspension) or ASD (automatic locking differential) – are not corroded. Open the boot and have a good look in the area where the spare wheel sits. Gently pull the plastic boot lining panels away and check behind them for corrosion, especially in the wells. Water can get into the boot, often from failed sunroof drain pipes or through the vents on the rear pillars. If it sits against the metal for long periods, it will eventually cause rust.

With the bonnet open, have a look for rust below the windscreen washer reservoir and underneath the radiator overflow pipe. Another common area for corrosion is the battery tray – you may have to move the battery or take it right out (with the owner's permission) to get a proper look.

ENGINE PROBLEMS

The four-cylinder petrol engines are generally considered extremely durable, although the 1.8-litre type is prone to head gasket failure: check for signs of overheating and of oil in the coolant. A rattle from the top of an M102 engine is usually caused by a worn timing chain, and the electric cooling fans sometimes give trouble. If the engine overheats, check that the fan is working correctly; if the engine seems to be under-cooled, the temperature sender unit may have failed and may be keeping the fan on all the time.

The six-cylinder engines have a reputation for racking up huge mileages, although they certainly can leak oil around the head gasket. On the related larger 3.0-litre six-cylinder (which was not available in the W201), head gaskets tend to give way at around 150,000 miles (241,000km). The 2.6-litre engines seem not to be as prone to this problem, but they cannot be considered immune to it either.

Later petrol models have catalytic converters in the exhaust and, as these are relatively expensive to replace, many owners will have avoided doing so. If the engine feels down on power and there is no other obvious reason, the catalytic converter may well be clogged and will need to be changed. A rattling sound when the engine is revved may suggest a different problem: the internals of the 'cat' may have been removed, either by an owner trying to save the cost of replacing a clogged one or by thieves cutting the canister open to remove the precious metals inside for resale as scrap. Take a close look to see if there is a cut in the casing, sometimes clumsily welded up.

When starting the engine, listen for an odd knocking sound that will probably die away fairly quickly. This may well be the result of a collapsed engine mounting (the hydraulic type often fails at around 150,000 miles; 241,000km), which allows the engine to knock against the sub-frame. You can confirm what it is by putting the steering on to full lock, when the problem causes a vibration.

The idling speed of most W201 engines, petrol and diesel alike, should be between 700 and 800rpm and should be steady; any lumpiness at idle suggests a problem that needs investigating. Typical causes are a faulty idle air control valve (IACV) and leaks in the rubber hoses of the injection system. The Cosworth engines usually idle a little higher than others, at around 900 to 1,000rpm, and in a cold engine the idle may be accompanied by a slight rattle that is known as 'cam clatter'. Check carefully that the noise is not actually timing-chain rattle.

GEARBOX AND DIFFERENTIAL PROBLEMS

Although there were multiple minor variations between models over the years, there were broadly four types of gearbox in the W201 models: a four-speed manual, a five-speed manual, a close-ratio five-speed manual (with dog's-leg change into first gear) and a four-speed automatic.

The automatic gearbox has a reputation for longevity and durability and is unquestionably the best choice for most models, except the Cosworth types, on which the close-ratio five-speed gives a much sportier driving experience. An automatic in good condition will give smooth changes. Any roughness in the driveline may be the result of worn propshaft 'doughnuts'. Check that the switch next to the gear lever really does select different Standard and Economy shift patterns; very early automatics did not have this feature.

The four-speed and overdrive five-speed gearboxes did have a change action that felt slow and rather vague, but they should not be so notchy that the lever has to be forced into a gear position. A really vague-feeling gearchange is probably in need of new bushes and possibly new linkages as well.

On a high-mileage car, do not be surprised to hear some differential whine. Although the differential may go on for

many thousands of miles without getting worse, it is as well to have this checked professionally and perhaps to factor in the cost of replacing the differential. (The whole operation is more complicated and expensive if an ASD system is fitted.) However, knocking noises from the differential at any mileage are a sign of a more serious problem and can certainly be used as a bargaining counter with the seller – if it does not put you off buying the car altogether.

INTERIOR PROBLEMS

The interior of a W201 tends to be hard-wearing. The cloth upholstery wears particularly well, but the velour trim (which was an extra-cost option and so uncommon) may well show more signs of age. This type of trim is quite costly to replace. Cars that have spent time in hot climates may also suffer from cracks in the dashboard.

Damp patches in the passenger cabin should always be thoroughly investigated. It is a good idea to lift the carpets to check for water sitting underneath them, as this will eventually rot through both the carpets and, more expensively, the floor panels if left unattended. Water typically gets into the car through a failed windscreen seal or sunroof drain (the pipes run through the A pillars and cannot be seen).

A leaking sunroof seal will cause discoloration or sagging of the headlining around the sun visors. It is also worth checking that the sunroof works properly, as this can seize up through lack of use. Other problems may be caused by a stripped gearwheel in the sunroof motor mechanism or by a break in the cable that moves the sunroof panel backwards and forwards.

If electric windows are fitted, make sure that they all work correctly. Water leaks may be a cause of failure, but it is also quite common to find that a break in the wire between the door pillar and the door itself is preventing the window responding to its switch. Also look closely at the door trims, which can lift away from the door at their top edges. It is impractical to check that all still have the transparent plastic rain sheet in place, but a damp or water-damaged door trim will usually indicate that the rain sheet has not been replaced properly – or at all.

Some cars have digital read-outs, such as an OTG (outside temperature gauge) or the stopwatch on the Cosworth models. These read-outs can deteriorate over the years, so it is worth checking that all the digits read clearly. The best solution is to replace a faulty unit.

There is not much still worth having in this scrapper, although the MB-Tex seats might be useful to somebody. FLICKR ©DAVE_7 FROM CANADA

Not really part of the interior, but operated from inside the car, is the windscreen wiper. Most cars have the 'jumping' type introduced in 1985, which wipes more of the screen than the original type (it is recognizable by a large plastic housing at the pivot end, which the early wiper does not have). Insufficient lubrication can cause wear in the eccentric that allows the wiper to 'jump'; this usually reveals itself as a noise when the wiper is in action. In more extreme cases, the mechanism can actually break. This will result in the wiper hitting the windscreen pillars and 'jumping' above the top of the windscreen.

Legroom in the rear is one of the car's weakest features. The front seats have been set well forward in this picture, to give the impression of more space in the back.

The 'jumping' windscreen wiper can give trouble if its gearing (carried in the centre) gets worn.

STEERING, SUSPENSION AND BRAKING PROBLEMS

Many people complain that the steering of a W201 feels lifeless; others find that it simply does its job unobtrusively. Most cars have the power-assisted variety, which is much nicer to use than the unassisted steering and, paradoxically perhaps, also feels rather more direct. The Cosworth cars and those with the Sportline option also have a quicker steering ratio, although the difference in feel is minimal.

The ride quality of a 190 is exemplary, although the handling is stodgy by more modern standards. It is nevertheless very safe and forgiving. It is worth checking that the rear of the car is not sagging, as springs can break; a knocking noise while driving may also suggest a broken spring. The Sportline cars with their lower ride height should feel much firmer on the road, but not uncomfortably so. On the Cosworth cars, make sure that there is a gap visible between the wheel arch and the top of the tyre, because a failed SLS system may cause the rear end to sit low. Conversely, an excessive height at the rear may also point to SLS trouble, and specifically to valve or accumulator failure.

On all cars fitted with the SLS system, check for leaks in the pipes that run under the car, check that there is fluid in the reservoir under the bonnet, and check around the engine-mounted pump for leaks as well.

AFTERMARKET PARTS

It was fashionable in the 1980s to dress up a car with wide wheels, bodykits and all manner of other items.

190s are not always what they appear. This derelict example was made to resemble a 16-valve Cosworth car at some stage, although it is actually a 2.0-litre model. The grille with three-pointed star is an aftermarket addition. CHARLIE, CC2.0

Although the major aftermarket converters of Mercedes (*see* Chapter 8) generally produced quality parts, their lesser imitators did not. Bodykits crack easily (and are not easy to repair); their fixings are sometimes rudimentary and can set up rust in the metal panels behind. Wide wheels and tyres put strain on wheel hubs and other components, and sometimes the standard Mercedes wheel bolts are only just long enough to engage with the threads in the hubs.

The message here is to be very cautious of cheap or DIY modifications. On the other hand, those done by the major specialists can generally be trusted. The only drawback to bear in mind is that replacement parts will be virtually unobtainable now.

The glamorous side of 190 ownership: an AMG-modified car. Unfortunately, it is rare to find survivors in good condition.

JOIN A CLUB

There are clubs for Mercedes-Benz enthusiasts all over the world, and the oldest among them is the British one (mercedes-benz.co.uk). There are also several online forums, clubs and groups dedicated to the marque in general and exclusively to the W201. The best advice is simply to browse through the options and to see what suits you. Being part of a group that shares your interests and problems is a very worthwhile part of classic car ownership, and is likely to save you money as well as find you some new friends!

Collecting sales literature for the W201 is a relatively inexpensive but enjoyable adjunct to ownership. However, the pictures will not always be fully representative of your car's original specification. The catalogues were prepared for global use, and specifications varied from one country to another.

OVERSEAS ASSEMBLY

Only one overseas Mercedes-Benz plant assembled W201 models, although the model was also cloned – somewhat ineffectually – in Asia.

South Africa
Close to the end of the W201's production cycle in Germany, the model was introduced in 190E 2.0 form in South Africa. However, these models were built from kits of parts shipped out from Germany, and were actually assembled at the South African Mercedes-Benz plant in East London. The car was launched in February 1993 and it appears that the entire build allocation had been sold by September 1993. There is no information available on quantities.

When *Car South Africa* magazine reported on a locally assembled 190E 2.0 automatic in its September 1993 edition, it was 'impressed that the car feels so refined, despite the fact that it was designed over a decade ago. There are shortcomings that show its age ... but other attributes, especially that splendid mix of steering feel and ride refinement, more than make up for this.'

North Korea
The Democratic People's Republic of Korea (North Korea) did not have an indigenous motor industry, but in the 1980s dictator Kim Il-Sung was keen to demonstrate that his country was just as capable as South Korea of manufacturing cars. On 10 April 1987 he issued a public declaration to that effect. One result of this was that several Mercedes W201s were imported in approximately 1987 and were reverse-engineered in North Korea.

The resulting car was known as a Kaengsaeng 88, and was built by the Pyongsang Auto Works in Pyongsang; it is also known as a Pyongsang 4.10, the numbers reflecting the date of Kim Il-Sung's declaration. However, it seems certain that the car did not get beyond the prototype stage. Very few examples have ever been seen, much less photographed, and North Korean officials have always preferred larger cars anyway; the rest of the population is too poor to afford cars, which are normally conferred on individuals as gifts of the state.

Only two photographs of the Kaengsaeng 88 are known in the West. One was taken in the capital city of Pyongyang in 1989 (by the German aristocrat Meinhard, Freiherr von Ow), and the other is of unknown origin but clearly shows a different car and has appeared on Flickr. The car is generally considered to have been a very poor copy of the original, distinguished by a different grille.

This North Korean Kaengsaeng 88 is one of only two known in the West.

IDENTIFICATION AND NUMBERING

CAR NUMBERS

Each W201 is identified by an individual VIN (Vehicle Identification Number). Mercedes used two types of VINs, one for the USA and one for the rest of the world. In both cases, the number is stamped into a plate on the bonnet slam panel and also into the bulkhead at the rear left of the engine bay (the right when standing in front of the car).

Standard international VINs

These VINs consist of seventeen digits, of which a (theoretical) example might be:

WDB2011221A654321.

This can be decoded as follows:

Digits 1–3	WDB	Manufacturer code (Mercedes-Benz)
Digits 4–6	201	Basic model type
Digits 7–9	122	Model variant (for full list, *see* below)
Digit 10		1 = LHD
		2 = RHD
		5 = LHD CKD
		6 = RHD CKD
Digit 11	A	Built at Sindelfingen
		A to E = Sindelfingen
		F to H = Bremen
Digits 12–17	654321	Serial number

US-style VINs

These VINs also consist of seventeen digits, but several positions in the alphanumeric string are used for different purposes. A (theoretical) example might be:

WDBDB26D4JF-543210.

This decodes as follows:

WDB	Manufacturer code (Daimler-Benz, Mercedes car division)
D	W201
B	Diesel
	A = petrol
26	Model code (this is a shortened form of the type code, in this case 201.126 for a 190D 2.5; *see* full list below)
D	Single airbag
	F = Airbag plus belt tensioners
4	Check digit
J	Model-year (1988)

	D = 1983	K = 1989	
	E = 1984	L = 1990	
	F = 1985	M = 1991	
	G = 1986	N = 1993	
	H = 1987	P = 1993	
F	Built at Bremen		
	A to E = Sindelfingen		
	F to H = Bremen		
	543210 Serial number		

The full list of car identification codes is:

Code	Type	Model	Production
201.018	W201 E 18	190E 1.8	1990–1993
201.023	W201 V 20/1	190	1984–1991
201.024	W 201 E 20	190E/190E 2.0	1982–1993
201.024	W201 E 23	190E 2.3	1983–1984
201.028	W201 E 23	190E 2.3	Sep 1984–1993
201.029	W201 E 26	190E 2.6	1986–1993
201.034	W201 E 23/2	190E 2.3-16	1984–1988
201.035	W201 E 25/2	190E 2.5-16	1988–1993
201.036	W 201 E 25/2	190E 2.5-16 Evolution I	1989
201.036	W201 E 25/2	190E 2.5-16 Evolution II	1990
201.122	W201 D 20	190D	1982–1993
201.122	W201 D 22	190D 2.2	1983–1985
201.126	W201 D 25	190D 2.5	1985–1993
201.128	W201 D 25A	190D 2.5 Turbo	1986–1993

ENGINE NUMBERS

The engine identification number will be stamped into the cylinder block below the inlet manifold near the front of the engine. Engines have a type identifier prefix that is followed by a serial number, typically with eight digits. The type identifiers are as follows (note that the KE letters are not stamped on the engine):

Code	Type	Model	Production
102.910 KE	M102 E 18	190E 1.8	1990–1993
102.924	M102 V 20	190	1984–1991
102.961 KE	M102 E23	190E 2.3	1983–Aug 1985
102.962 KE	M102 E 20	190E/190E 2.0	1982–1993
102.983 KE	M102 E 23/2	190E 2.3-16	1984–1988
102.985 KE	M102 E 20	190E 2.3	Sep 1985–1993
102.990 KE	M102 E 25/2	190E 2.5-16	1988–1993
102.991 KE	M102 E 25/2	190E 2.5-16 Evolution I	1989
102.992 KE	M102 E 25/2	190E 2.5-16 Evolution II	1990
103.942 KE	M103 E 26	190E 2.6	1986–1993
103.983	M103 E 32	190E 3.2 AMG	1992–1993
601.911	OM601 D 20	190D	1983–1993
601.921	OM601 D 22	190D 2.2	1983–1985
602.911	OM602 D 25	190D 2.5	1985–1993
602.961	OM602 D 25 A	190D 2.5 Turbo	1986–1993

GEARBOX NUMBERS

The gearbox type identifier is stamped on a machined surface on the gearbox casing. The identifiers are as follows:

Code	Type	Configuration	Model	Production
716.212	GL68/20 C	4sp manual	190E	1982–1983
716.213	GL68/20 D	4sp manual	190D	1983–1993
716.216	GL68/20 G	4sp manual	190	1984–1988
716.216	GL68/20 G	4sp manual	190E	1983–1988
716.217	GL68/20 H	4sp manual	190	1988–1991
716.217	GL68/20 H	4sp manual	190E 1.8	1990–1993
716.217	GL68/20 H	4sp manual	190E/190E 2.0	1988–1993
717.404	GL275 E	5sp close-ratio manual	190E 2.3-16	1984–1988
717.404	GL275 E	5sp close-ratio manual	190E 2.5-16	1988–1993
717.404	GL275 E	5sp close-ratio manual	190E 2.5-16 Evolution I	1989
717.404	GL275 E	5sp close-ratio manual	190E 2.5-16 Evolution II	1989
717.410	GL68/20 A-5	5sp manual	190D	1983–1985
717.410	GL68/20 A-5	5sp manual	190D 2.2	1983–1985
717.411	GL68/20 B-5	5sp manual	190D	1985–1988
717.411	GL68/20 B-5	5sp manual	190D 2.5	1985–1989
717.411	GL68/20 B-5	5sp manual	190	1984–1989
717.411	GL68/20 B-5	5sp manual	190E	1982–1989
717.411	GL68/20 B-5	5sp manual	190E 2.3	1983–1988
717.412	GL68/20 C-5	5sp manual	190D	1988–1989
717.412	GL68/20 C-5	5sp manual	190D 2.5	1989–1993
717.412	GL68/20 C-5	5sp manual	190	1989–1991
717.412	GL68/20 C-5	5sp manual	190E 1.8	1990–1993
717.412	GL68/20 C-5	5sp manual	190E/190E 2.0	1989–1993
717.412	GL68/20 C-5	5sp manual	190E 2.3	1988–1989
717.413	GL68/20 D-5	5sp manual	190E 2.3	1989–1993
717.413	GL68/20 F-5	5sp manual	190D	1989–1993
717.413	GL68/20 F-5	5sp manual	190D 2.5	1989–1993
717.432	GL76/27 C-5	5sp manual	190E 2.6	1988–1993
717.435	GL76/27 F-5	5sp manual	190E 2.6	1986–1988
717.437	GL76/27 F-5	5sp manual	190D 2.5 Turbo	1989–1993

GEARBOX NUMBERS *(continued)*

Code	Type	Configuration	Model	Production
722.400	W4A 020	4sp automatic	190D 2.5 Turbo	1986–1988
722.400	W4A 020	4sp automatic	190E/190E 2.0	1982–1993
722.400	W4A 020	4sp automatic	190E 2.3	1983–1988
722.403	W4A 020	4sp automatic	190D	1983–1993
722.403	W4A 020	4sp automatic	190D 2.2	1983–1985
722.409	W4A 020	4sp automatic	190E 2.6	1986–1988
722.409	W4A 020	4sp automatic	190E 2.3	1988–1993
722.409	W4A 020	4sp automatic	190E 2.6	1988–1993
722.410	W4A 020	4sp automatic	190E 2.3-16	1986–1988
722.411	W4A 020	4sp automatic	190	1984–1991
722.413	W4A 020	4sp automatic	190D 2.5 Turbo	1988–1993
722.414	W4A 020	4sp automatic	190D 2.5	1985–1993
722.417	W4A 020	4sp automatic	190E 2.5-16	1988–1993
722.420	W4A 020	4sp automatic	190E 1.8	1990–1993

PRODUCTION FIGURES
FOR THE W201

According to Mercedes-Benz, the overall total of W201 models built between 1982 and 1993 was 1,879,629; the company often rounds it up to 1,879,630. It is unfortunately not clear whether that total includes cars that were built up overseas from CKD kits manufactured in Germany (see Appendix I).

    That total can be broken down as shown below. The figures are presented in descending order of magnitude.

190E/190E 2.0	638,180
190D	452,806
190E 2.3	186,610
190E 1.8	173,354
190D 2.5	147,502
190	118,561(*)
190E 2.6	104,907
190D 2.5 Turbo	20,915
190E 2.3-16	19,487
190D 2.2	10,560
190E 2.5-16	5,743
Evolution I	502
Evolution II	502

This figure can be broken down further into 35,021 cars built between 1982 and 1984 with the original engine, and 83,540 built between 1984 and 1991 with the revised engine.

The figures also provide a breakdown of petrol versus diesel types, which were as follows:

Petrol	1,247,846
Diesel	631,783

INDEX

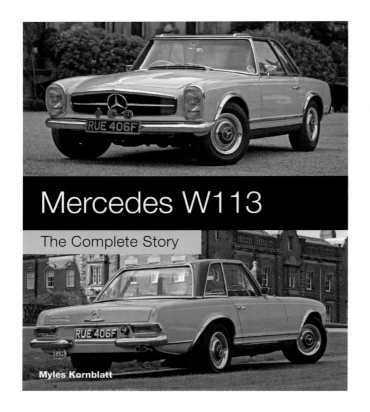
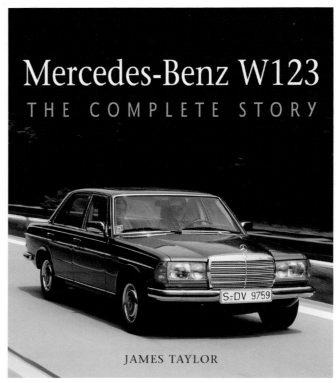
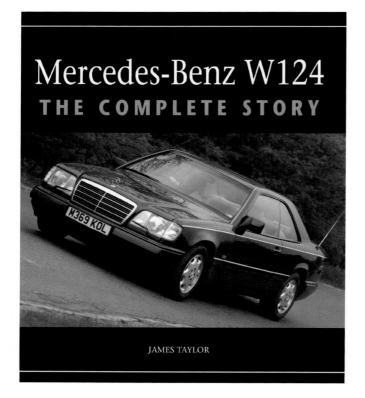
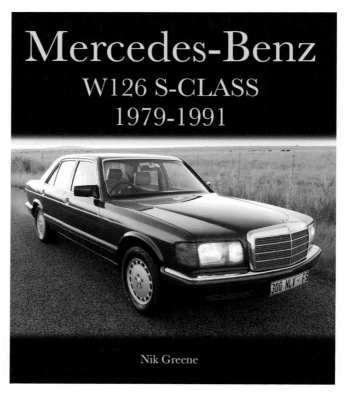